NEIL SIMON

NEIL SIMON
A Critical Study

Edythe M. McGovern

With Notes from the Playwright

FREDERICK UNGAR PUBLISHING CO.

NEW YORK

Publisher's Note

This is the second edition of a paperback book first published as
Not-So-Simple Neil Simon by Perivale Press, 13830 Erwin Street,
Van Nuys, California 91401. All orders for the paperback edition
should go directly to them. This volume retains all of the original
material, but to conserve paper the present edition has been completely repaged. New text and illustrations have been added, and
an entirely new index is also included.

Contents

Illustrations

Foreword

It has seemed to me for some years that Neil Simon is always discussed in terms of his popularity, his sure-fire "hits," with an emphasis on the commercial rewards of writing "entertainment for the tired business man." Perhaps it is a peculiarly American trait to offer adulation to people who "make it big," while at the same time tacitly accepting the notion that whatever material succeeds in our culture must of necessity be ephemeral and worthless. At any rate, seldom has even the most astute critic recognized what depths really exist in the plays of Neil Simon—some of them in particular.

Perhaps it is the genre in which he writes—comedy—which causes the problem. It is quite easy to see a comedy in terms only of its surface, especially since traditionally, comedy always ends happily. Furthermore, Neil Simon's plays *are* very, very funny. However, there has always been a select group of playwrights, and admittedly, they are an exclusive group in terms of talent as well as numbers, who have used this ancient form to make some very serious statements about the world and its inhabitants. Playwrights in the tradition of Ben Jonson, Molière, and George Bernard Shaw successfully raised fundamental and sometimes tragic issues of universal and therefore enduring interest without eschewing the comic mode, and it is my firm conviction that Neil Simon should be considered a member of this company. To my mind, close analysis of his work will make clear that an invitation to "join the club" is long overdue. Thus, a play-by-play discussion of thirteen non-musical theatrical works of Neil Simon.

Neil Simon — Photo by Gary Dontzig

Notes from the Playwright

Writing the twelve plays that are studied, analyzed, probed and scrutinized in Ms. McGovern's meticulous work did not seem as frightening for me as reading her critical appraisal. Putting a play like *Come Blow Your Horn,* my first effort (it took three years to write and twenty complete new versions), under today's microscope with all its advanced technology, is like looking at a yellowed and faded photograph of ourselves in a tattered family album and saying, "My God, did I really look like that when I was a kid? Did I really wear knickers with long socks and part my hair straight down the middle like a turn-of-the-century Third Avenue bartender?" . . . Sixteen years' work passed through Ms. McGovern's discerning lens, and reading it through in one sitting shook me up. I never re-read my old plays, but doing it through intelligent purely clinical eyes, it was enormously revealing to me. When I was good, I was very, very good . . . and when I was bad, we folded.

Come Blow Your Horn, for me, in the time it was written, seemed like a monumental effort. Today, it seems like the crude markings in a cave by the first prehistoric chronicler. Still, it was an important step for me. The theater and I discovered each other. I was in love, and she would one day be mine, no matter how many rewrites it took. It took a lot.

How much of Ms. McGovern's analysis do I agree with? A great deal. I was and am very fond of *Barefoot in the Park.* A light and delicate play that seems so easy to do and yet can be more difficult to bring off than weightier subjects. "Hard earned simplicity is the keynote," to quote, I believe, Oscar Hammerstein II. . . . A big thanks to director Mike Nichols for bringing it off.

The Odd Couple, for the most part, is a sound play. The seams show a bit in the third act. I rewrote it five times out of town. I think I needed one more town. *Star Spangled Girl* is clearly and simply a failure, as far as I'm concerned. It's the only play I ever wrote where I did not have a clear visual image of the characters in my mind as I sat down at the typewriter. Walter Kerr wisely wrote, "Neil Simon didn't have an idea for a play this year, but he wrote it anyway." Thank you, Walter. The following year I had an idea. *Plaza Suite*. "Visitors from Mamaroneck" in particular achieved new directions for me: dealing with serious subject matter, and treating it with humor and compassion. I was not yet ready to tackle a full length play in this vein, but this one acter was a good beginning.

I like a lot of *Last of the Red Hot Lovers*. It is not modesty that makes me say "a lot of." I have never written a play that I thought was completely satisfying. The playwright has obligations to fulfill, such as exposition and character building that must be done. The trick is to do it skillfully. One is always so eager to get to the "meat," or the confrontations between the antagonist and protagonist, that one occasionally skimps on details. The mature playwright rarely skimps. I am in the process of maturing.

The Gingerbread Lady is a faulty play, but one of my favorites. Lillian Hellman bitterly learned as a young playwright the pitfalls of trying to mix comedy with tragedy. I have held fast to the belief that if it happens in life, why can't it happen on the stage? With all its faults, I think *The Gingerbread Lady* is a better play than critics would have us believe, as Ms. McGovern has concluded. In any event, it led me into uncharted waters where I discovered new directions for the future.

The Prisoner of Second Avenue was the result of those new directions. It is an intricate play with the usual second act blues. Mel's paranoia scene and the sudden introduction of his family may not be fine weaving at its best, but it served its purpose for me. I am fond of *The Prisoner of Second Avenue*.

The Sunshine Boys, dealing with old age and its inevitable crisis, may not be the most popular subject for your average theater goer, but for me, it was the best work I had done to date. Structurally it was sound, and its character delineation was accurate. I spent my life growing up with these men. If they spoke in one-liners and punch lines instead of conversation, it's because it was the only language they knew. Spend a few afternoons around the Friars Club, a hangout for aging comedians, and a pencil, a pad, and a discriminating ear will record for you some of the funniest and saddest dialogue you ever heard. A good play, *The Sunshine Boys*.

Sad to say, *God's Favorite* was not. Not because of its subject matter, a contemporary version through this play-wright's oblique viewpoint of the Book of Job, but because it was simply not done skillfully enough. When you tackle God, you'd better be up for it.

The Good Doctor, of course, is not a play at all. There are sketches, vaudeville scenes, if you will, written with my non-consenting collaborator, Anton Chekhov. Not the Chekhov of *The Sea Gull* and *The Three Sisters*, but the young man who wrote humorous articles for the newspapers to pay his way through medical school. It was a pastiche for me, an enjoyable interlude before getting on to bigger things. It was, to digress for a moment, a joyous experience for me. I met my wife doing this one. Some of the scenes worked; others didn't. The marriage, I'm glad to say, did.

California Suite again brings me back to the short one act form. The audiences responded most to "Visitors from Philadelphia." It is, as Ms. McGovern points out, pure Feydeau. That was its intention. I was more interested in form than content. It's very funny, I most humbly submit, but for me, the best piece of short form writing I've ever done is in "Visitors from London." I think it's because these were people not from out of my own experience, as I had taken in the past, but from people out of my observation. I felt as though I had moved from doing still lifes to landscapes, seeing a broader view of life. Self portraits are no less demanding, but it's nice to know what the other fellow is thinking about once in a while.

I wish to thank Edythe McGovern for her skillful and dedicated efforts to give the comic playwright a serious retrospective . . . or, for that matter, giving a serious playwright a comic retrospective. Since, hopefully, there will be more plays in the future, we can sort out the difference at a later date.

NEIL SIMON
Los Angeles
Nov. 7th, 1977

Overview

There are any number of time-honored critical approaches from which to choose when undertaking an analysis of works written for the theatre. From Aristotle to Artaud, many thoughtful people involved with the dramatic arts have been concerned with setting down criteria on which to base judgments about plays. Indeed, as every advanced student of theatre can attest, there are as many ways to evaluate plays as there are writers who attempt evaluation, and only occasionally is there the slightest iota of agreement among them as to the most valid method of formulating objective conclusions.

On one point, however, most theatrical experts do agree. This is true because there is irrefutable evidence to support the contention that tragedies and serious dramas generally maintain their value for a far greater time than comedies. There are two rather obvious reasons for this longevity. First, comedy frequently rests on a consideration of trivia which quickly becomes tiresome, and, secondly, there is the pitfall of topicality. When based only on what makes us laugh today, a play will no longer interest us when its subject matter becomes yesterday's news. If this topicality has been written into a piece for the theatre, so that it is intrinsic to it, it is quite likely that the play's life will be rather short and totally undistinguished.

Nevertheless, some comedies have survived the test of time. What then is the common ingredient found in plays which have continued to interest audiences for hundreds of years? Even a cursory study of the works of such acknowledged masters of comedy as Ben Jonson, Molière, and George Bernard Shaw reveals the answer: *characters*. People are always interested in other people, which translated to literary terms means that they are interested in characters. Perhaps because of what is commonly called identification with other human beings, most of us can easily become involved with what may baldly be termed "gossip," whether it is a bit of news about those we know personally or those we feel we know simply because we have seen them as entertainers, sports stars, or politicians. Below (or possibly above) this level of surface interest in others, we also become involved in other people's emotions, problems, weaknesses and strengths, foibles and idiocyncrasies—whatever may be revealing about the human condition. If we accept the premise that not only in life, but also in literature, characters engender interest, then we can easily agree that a literary work which has characters who capture the reader or viewer is on its way to achieving the quality of universality,[1] which in turn signifies that it will have wide appeal and be likely to maintain that appeal for a long time.

Now, this is not to say that characters, universal though they may be, may not also be somewhat exaggerated. It is a truism that art is not synonymous with reality, but is only a representation of it. Therefore, we accept the fact that noteworthy tragic characters, particularly those created for the stage, must be "larger than life." Whether we are considering the characterization of Medea or Oedipus, Lear or Hamlet, St. Joan of Arc or Blanche DuBois, Cyrano or Willie Loman, there is this slightly enlarged quality about all of them which is entirely acceptable as long as it does not preclude audience identification. The same principle holds true for characters drawn in the comic mode by the great playwrights in that genre: Jonson, Molière or Shaw. What none of these creations can be, however, if they are to achieve universal appeal is "manipulated." That is, if they do not ultimately behave in a manner logical for them, as drawn by their creators, we dismiss them as one-dimensional, flat, cardboard, unoriginal, or so completely predictable as to be at the very best, dull.[2]

If, however, the artist does not manipulate his characters, but allows them free rein to evolve in their own way, to behave as people would behave, given certain personalities and a particular set of circumstances, we can empathize and "willingly suspend the disbelief"[3] with which we enter the theatre. To underscore this point, let us examine a few classic comic characters created by Jonson, Molière and Shaw.

Ben Jonson's early plays were direct satires against specific personages involved in the "War of the Theatres"[4], but in *The Silent Woman, The Alchemist,* and *Volpone* he reached his height as a playwright who used the comic mode to reveal human weakness and chicanery. For instance, in *Volpone* (subtitled *The Fox*), the protagonist is a reprehensible man who pretends over and over to be on his deathbed in order to profit from the deeply rooted greed of other men. His plan succeeds; each of his "friends" is so possessed by the idea of being named the sole heir that he will give Volpone everything from material gifts to a son's inheritance, or even a beautiful young wife. Jonson, no matter how exaggerated these characters are, never has them behave in ways which are illogical for them. Furthermore, when Volpone finally has an opportunity to go scot free (and he has behaved evilly himself, of course), he succumbs to the temptation to do just one more trick, completely in keeping with what such a man would do, so that he is punished by being sent to prison and "The Fox is mortified."[5] If frequent, successful revival is any criterion, this play must certainly be counted as a classic. And there are others.

No playwright, with the exception of Shakespeare (whose romantic comedies are quite different from the type under discussion here) has known more success over the past four hundred years than Molière. His plays are filled with characters so nearly monomaniacal as to be almost caricatures. In *The Imaginary Invalid,* for instance, he has created Argan, a man so far into his own hypochondria that he will go to any lengths to marry his unwilling daughter to a "doctor" so that he may be guaranteed medical attention. In *Tartuffe* he has given us not only the title character, the epitome of a hypocrite, but also Orgon, whose faith in the charlatan Tartuffe overshadows all his reasonable family relationships. In *The Miser* he has drawn Harpagon, a man so concerned with his money that when it is stolen, he suspects everybody, even himself! Who has ever read or seen this play and can forget the speech delivered to the audience at the end of Act IV when the miser discovers that his money box is missing:

Stop thief! Stop thief! Stop assassin! Stop murderer! Justice, Divine Justice! I am ruined! I've been murdered! He cut my throat, he stole my money! Who can it be? . . . Who's this? (*sees his own shadow and grabs his own arm*). Stop! Give me back my money, you rogue. Ah, it is myself. My mind is unhinged, and I don't know where I am, who I am or what I am doing. (*lies down*) I am dying. I am dead. I am buried! Isn't there anybody who would like to bring me back to life by returning my dear money or by telling me who took it? I'll order them to torture everyone in my house for a confession: the maids, the valets, my son, my daughter—and myself too! (*addresses audience on his knees*) Please, if anyone has any information about my thief, I beg you to tell me. Are you sure he isn't hidden there among you? They all look at me and laugh. . . I want to have everybody hanged. And if I don't recover my money, I'll hang myself afterward![6]

Completely ridiculous? Certainly. But because of the consistency of Harpagon's character, as a man who puts his money above even his own life, there is verisimilitude and universality.

Coming closer to our own time, George Bernard Shaw's characters often seem destined to drown in their own oceans of words, so anxious (and occasionally obvious) is the playwright to get his ideas across to the audience. Because of this torrent of words, so often part of Shavian creations, they are frequently exaggerations. However, the playwright gives a sense of reality even to a character such as Undershaft in *Major Barbara* by first convincing us that he is quite capable of speaking as he does. Therefore, when his son, Stephen, asserts that men like Undershaft and his ilk can be controlled by laws made in a democratic government body, it is plausible for the self-made munitions maker to reply:

The government of your country! I am the government of your country: I and Lazarus. Do you suppose that you and a half a dozen amateurs like you, sitting in a row in that foolish gabble shop, can govern Undershaft and Lazarus? No, my friend: you will do what pays us. You will make war when it suits us, and keep peace when it doesn't. You will find out that trade requires certain measures when we have decided on those measures. When I want anything to keep my dividends up, you will discover that my want is a national need. When other people want something to keep my dividends down, you will call out the police and the military. And in return you shall have the support and applause of my newspapers and the delight of imagining that you are a great statesman. Be off with you, my boy, and play with your caucuses and leading articles and historical parties and great leaders and burning questions and the rest of your toys. I am going back to my counting-house to pay the piper and call the tune.[7]

So we believe that it is entirely possible for this character, as he has been created by the playwright, to answer thus, although we may at the same time be intellectually aware that Undershaft is acting as a raison d'être to justify Shaw's Fabian Socialism.

In much the same way, some of Neil Simon's characters may be exaggerated at times while still remaining plausible because of an inner consistency given them by the playwright. They are usually amusing the audience with sparkling "zingers," which are obviously not always completely realistic, but his people are so skillfully done that they are not only delightful to watch, hear, and laugh with, but also very believable. And this is important because through them the playwright deals with some serious and continuing concerns of mankind—some important themes, if you will—rather than with purely topical material which can only elicit transitory laughter.

And what are some of the subjects which seem important to Neil Simon? Not openly autobiographical, like Eugene O'Neill or Tennessee Williams, Simon's work shows a great deal about the man—his background, value system and substance. He does not deal with people he has not known intimately, such as the lowest echelons of society; he has little to say about the very affluent, unless they are in the theatre. His characters are sometimes Jewish, but only nominally so.[8] He makes little comment on race relations. Basically, he holds with conventional societal patterns common in the liberal segments of the middle class. Surprisingly, he might be considered somewhat sexist by some women libbers, since most of his female characters are conforming housewives, who assert themselves only rarely, and those women not cast in this mold are, generally speaking, quite unhappy. His plays are filled with frustrated people, although only occasionally does a character border on the neurotic. He is very concerned about family relationships and deals with some of the problems most common in this area: sibling rivalry, prejudgment of one generation by another, marital infidelity, and divorce. On a social level, there is frequently conflict between the standards of behavior considered acceptable to middle class Americans before the 1960's and the freer attitudes of the same group today. There is always impatience with phoniness, with shallowness, with amorality. And there is certainly some implicit and explicit criticism of modern urban life with its stress, its vacuity, and its materialism.

Neil Simon's characters are often middle-aged, and he does not overlook what psychologists have come to recognize as "the crisis years." However, he also deals with the quite young and the very old. No matter how unfortunate or even occasionally evil his characters may be, he has great sympathy for them. There is always in his work an implied seeking for solutions to human problems through relationships with other people, despite the ineptness with which some of his characters attempt to make such connections. Above all, there is a willingness to "live and let live," or even help live, so that Neil Simon does not carp like Jonson, snipe like Molière, nor preach like Shaw, but seems to affirm in Barney Cashman's words, "We're not indecent, we're not unloving, we're human. That's what we are, *human*."[9] It is this quality which comes through to some extent in all of his work and very strongly in the best of it. Through expert character delineation, Neil Simon is able to deal with serious topics of universal and enduring concern, while stimulating the only animal with the capacity to laugh to exercise that capability with gusto.

1. Universality is a critical term frequently employed to indicate the presence in a piece of writing of an appeal to all readers of all time. This usually indicates that the writing presents the great human emotions common to all people: jealousy, love, pride, and so on.

2. Such characterizations are seen on many TV shows almost constantly, and a few exist in some plays of even the foremost playwrights. For example, unless minor characters have a definite function to fulfill plotwise, or have a role in revealing the playwright's theme, they are frequently drawn as "stock characters," which means that they are little more than animate props.

3. Samuel Taylor Coleridge, *Biographia Literaria,* A. Symons, ed. (London, 1906), Chapter 14.

4. This refers to rivalries among theatrical companies and their members during the period of Elizabethan drama, prior to 1600.

5. Ben Jonson, *Complete Plays, Vol. I* (London, New York, 1910), Scene VIII, p. 487.

6. Molière, *The Miser,* Lloyd C. Parks, trans. (Denton, Texas, 1951).

7. George Bernard Shaw, *Major Barbara* (London, 1905), Act III, Lines 416-439.

8. When religion enters at all, as in *God's Chosen,* it is on quite a different level. Generally, it is not an issue with Simon.

9. Neil Simon, *Last of the Red Hot Lovers* (New York, 1970), Act III.

Come Blow Your Horn

First presented at Brooks Atkinson Theatre, New York City, by William Hammerstein and Michael Ellis, February 22, 1961.

Director: Stanley Prager

Setting and Lighting: Ralph Alswang

Costumes: Stanley Simmons

CAST

Alan Baker	Hal March
Peggy Evans	Arlene Golonka
Buddy Baker	Warren Berlinger
Mr. Baker	Lou Jacobi
Connie Dayton	Sarah Marshall
Mrs. Baker	Pert Kelton
A Visitor	Carolyn Brenner

Number of Performances: 677

Come Blow Your Horn — Photo by Joseph Abeles Studio
(Actors, left to right) Sarah Marshall, Hal March, Pert
Kelton, Warren Berlinger, Lou Jacobi

Come Blow Your Horn (1961)

As the title of his first full-length play Neil Simon used a line from a nursery rhyme and cleverly worked out the idea that although "Little Boy Blue" in the character of Alan Baker might be flagrantly neglectful of his duties at the opening of the piece, he would become very conscientious by the end. Amusingly, his younger brother, Buddy Baker, first seen as a really naive and earnest young man, exchanges roles with Alan, which puts this play into the category of a "well-made" French farce, à la Feydeau. As a matter of fact, most of the action is, technically speaking, divided into "French scenes," which means that as one character leaves, another enters, and a new "scene" is under way. However, despite some character manipulation and more plotting for its own sake than he uses in later plays, at least one serious idea does come through: the significance of the family as a unit.

The first act opens as Alan Baker and a "friend," Peggy Evans, are returning from a ski trip to Vermont where Alan was supposed to have introduced her to a Mr. Manheim, a producer from MGM in Hollywood. The girl establishes her IQ at once by thinking they had been to New Hampshire because she's "terrible with names." It becomes obvious at once that there is no such person as Manheim and that there had been little skiing done as well. Alan, quite ready to continue their "sport" at his apartment temporarily gets rid of the girl just before his twenty-one year old brother arrives and announces that he has left the parental nest to become a "swinging bachelor" too.

We are then given a graphic picture of the family and particularly of the elder Mr. Baker in a series of hilarious lines exchanged between the brothers, and we also learn that both sons are involved in their father's business, the manufacture of

waxed fruit, a product appropriate to the man's rigidity. Buddy
wants "out" because as he says,

> Gee whiz, there's a million more important things going on in
> the world today. . . . It's different for you, Alan. You're hardly
> ever there. You're the salesman; you're outside all day.
> Meeting people. Human beings. But I'm inside, looking at
> petrified apples and pears and plums. They never rot, they
> never turn brown, they never grow old. It's like the fruit version
> of 'The Picture of Dorian Gray.'

His older brother assures him that dealing with waxed fruit
during the day can be made bearable if one bites into the *real*
fruit of life at night, and Buddy agrees that even living where he
won't be forced to "have milk and cake standing over the sink"
will be a pleasant change.

As Buddy samples his Scotch and ginger ale (!), his mother
calls, and we hear from his conversation that she has had the
great idea of tearing up his Declaration of Independence letter
before his father comes home to read it, particularly since the
elder Mr. Baker has already called to tell her that Alan has
alienated a valued customer, Mr. Meltzer, by not showing up
for an appointment. Buddy is almost ready to renounce his new
freedom and return to the old homestead, but Alan persuades
him to stay by reminding him that at sixty-five he will get social
security, not girls.

Since Alan expects the imminent return of Peggy, he is
surprised to find that the next ring of the doorbell signals the
entry of a scowling father instead. Buddy secretly disappears
into the bedroom, and we get a very pithy dialogue between
Harry Baker and his elder son. It is really a verbal attack on
Alan, punctuated at regular intervals by Harry screaming,
"BUM!" Nevertheless, even this early, Neil Simon manages to
make a point in an exchange which goes like this:

ALAN: . . . What good does it do coming in? You don't need
           me. You never ask my advice about the business, do
           you?
FATHER: What does a skier know about waxed fruit?
ALAN: You see. You see. You won't even listen.

FATHER: Come in early. I'll listen.
ALAN: I did. For three years. Only then I was 'too young' to
         have anything to say. And now that I've got my own
         apartment, I'm too much of a 'bum' to have any-
         thing to say. Admit it, Dad. You don't give me the
         same respect you give the night watchman.

Although this last line is the signal for a joke, as Harry replies,
"At least I know where he is nights," there is some slight
indication of the way a patriarch like Harry Baker behaves
toward his children. Furthermore, Harry's contention that if one
is past thirty and unmarried, he is automatically a wastrel is also
a familiar attitude taken by the older generation, particularly
within groups in which family life is held in high esteem. Next,
Mr. Baker holds Buddy up as a shining example of a "good
son," which is not an uncommon device used by parents who
compare their wayward children to other more worthy members
of the family, in a mistaken attempt to improve the behavior of
those who displease them. Finally, the father exits with a great
malapropism: "The day your brother becomes like you, I throw
myself in front of an airplane."

This remark causes Buddy to rush out from his hiding place,
ready to telephone his mother and have his farewell letter
destroyed before his father sees it and takes drastic action.
Alan, however, has other plans. He telephones Mr. Meltzer,
tells him blatant lies about having mistakenly been in Atlantic
City with "the girls" that he'd promised to have for this
customer, and then promises that he'll "deliver" almost
immediately. He then amazes his brother by securing
(procuring?) a certain Chickie Parker and her French roommate
to meet him at Meltzer's room at the Hotel Croyden in half an
hour. An astounded and impressed Buddy remarks, "And it
took me three months to get a date for my prom."

Everything seems to be going smoothly for the moment, but
in the manner of a French farce, a complication arises almost at
once when Connie Dayton announces her arrival by intercom
from the lobby. Even before her entry, it is apparent that she
will be a contrast to Alan's usual one-night stands, such as the
nubile Peggy Evans, since Alan explains to his young brother

that Connie is a really *nice* girl. He admits, "She's different. She's not like. . . . Well, she's different." However, when Buddy suggests that this admission may be taken as indicative of Alan's finally becoming "serious," he is promptly disabused of that notion. Alan quickly explains, "Who said serious? I just said *different.*" He then goes on to make it clear that his intentions toward Connie are strictly dishonorable, as he waves off his brother's notion that marriage is a possibility. "Married?" he says, "Me? With all this? Are you crazy? She's the *nicest,* but I'm working on it," implying, of course, that Connie won't remain a "nice" girl any longer than Alan can help it.

In the scene which follows Connie's entrance, the dialogue makes both sense and fun, but Simon does not come up to his later skill in characterization since what ensues is a kind of transparent foreshadowing of Alan's third-act capitulation to become the kind of man his parents want him to become— married, with a responsible attitude toward the "sheep in the meadow." At any rate, Connie tells Alan that she is quitting her traveling jobs in industrial shows in favor of remaining in New York, to be near him. At the same time, she gives him an ultimatum. If he wants her to have an affair with him, she will; if he wants her to marry him, she will. As he says, "If I say I want you, you're mine. If I say I love you, I'm yours." He tries to shock her by choosing the "march into the bedroom" over the "march down the aisle," but as she exits, she goes him one better by saying that she will return. She says, "I just figure if I'm going into business here I might as well get the rest of my merchandise."

Surprised or not, Alan must leave to keep his date with the customer (Meltzer) and the fun-girls, so he talks Buddy into accepting Peggy for the evening.[1] Buddy is supposed to play the part of the non-existent Mr. Manheim, and after Alan leaves, he's obviously frightened at the thought of what's to come. Neil Simon, however, bails him out, for when the doorbell rings, it is not Peggy waiting for admittance to Alan's replica of Sodòm and Gomorrah, but Mrs. Baker, his mother.

Act II continues the action and we find that Mrs. Baker is a well-meaning, but constantly agitated and agitating woman.

She is almost a "stock" character, the mother who is concerned about little in life which isn't within the orbit of her family's welfare, but who, at the same time, manages to irritate rather than soothe because she is so sincerely over-solicitous. She is worried about her husband's reaction to Buddy's leaving. As she puts it:

> I know what he's going to say tonight. He'll blame it all on me. He'll say I was too easy with both of you. He'll say 'Because of you my sister Gussie has two grandchildren and all I've got is a *bum* and a *letter.*' I know him.

Finally, in desperation because he fears that Peggy will arrive before his mother leaves, Buddy goes downstairs to get a taxi-cab to return his mother to what her sons call "The Museum of Expensive Furniture." This interval gives the playwright (and the actress playing the role) an opportunity to do what amounts to almost a complete vaudeville sketch, since the telephone rings constantly, and Mrs. Baker tries valiantly but in vain to take messages. The reason? She cannot find a pencil anywhere, and so she gets everything hopelessly and hilariously mixed up. She finally ends by screaming into the phone, "Hello? What do you want? Who is this? Alan who? Oh, Alan. . ." and starts to cry, handing the phone to the breathless Buddy, who, of course, cannot straighten things out since he has been absent during his mother's time "playing secretary." The audience, however, has been given an inkling of future plot complications from what Mrs. Baker has said to the first caller, Mr. Meltzer, who does *not* want Alan to come to the Hotel Croyden with "those certain parties" since his wife has come in unexpectedly from Atlantic City and then to a second caller, Chickie Parker, who wants to be sure that she was to go to the Croyden Hotel.

Buddy adds to the confusion by telling Alan that he is not going to play Mr. Manheim for Peggy. When he starts to write her a note to this effect—in Alan's name—he comes up with a container of about two dozen pencils! He does not get away, however, before Peggy arrives, and the scene between these two once again borders on old-time vaudeville, with remarks made by each person being misinterpreted by the other. For example,

PEGGY: Well, now- down to business. I suppose you want to know what I've done.

BUDDY: Not necessarily.

PEGGY: I'll be perfectly frank with you. I've never been in a picture before.

BUDDY: Is that so?

PEGGY: But I'm not totally inexperienced.

BUDDY: So Alan told me.

PEGGY: Last summer when I was on the Coast, I did an "Untouchables."

BUDDY: No kidding?

PEGGY: I was a dead body. They fished me out of the river.

BUDDY: I think I saw that.

PEGGY: Lots of people did. I got loads of work from it. But it's not what I really want to do. That's why I'm taking acting class with Felix Ungar. He lives in this building. Right under this apartment. In fact, that's how I met Alan. I rang the wrong bell one night.[2]

The next interruption comes when Harry Baker makes his second appearance, but by now the character of Buddy has begun to change so that he's able to lie more smoothly to get Peggy out of the way before he attempts to deal with his father. This kind of personality change coming as it does within four pages of script is typical of farce, but not really well motivated in the manner of the later Neil Simon. At any rate, the conversation between Harry and his younger son is very humorous, and here the playwright redeems himself somewhat by making some really telling points of character. Buddy's father cannot understand why his son wants to be independent at the age of twenty-one, and when Buddy respectfully reminds him that at the same age he had been a married man, Harry's retort is perfectly in character for a first-generation American who has "worked his way up through the school of hard knocks." He says, "Those days were altogether different. I was working when I was eleven years old. I didn't go to camp." Of course, it's a non sequitur, but it is very revealing of the feelings held by many members of the older generation when considering the attitudes of their children. Buddy tries to explain without much success that perhaps the "biggest artificial fruit manufacturing house in the East" isn't the right field for him, that he may want to be a writer, an idea which his father turns into a joke about his being a writer of letters. There may be a serious note here, however, since Buddy says he wants to try to write plays for the theatre or for television and his father answers, "Plays can close. Television you turn off. Wax fruit lays in the bowl till you're a hundred." Whether or not this conversation is in any way connected to the playwright's life is immaterial, but it certainly is an exchange which comes out of very realistic characterizations. We can also understand that Buddy, who is twelve years younger than Alan, was always an obedient, somewhat shy, introverted child, whereas Alan apparently spent his childhood as a comparatively self-willed, extroverted youngster. In any case, just as Buddy has persuaded his father to "trust him," at least overnight, Peggy barges in and ruins everything.

Since Buddy had told the girl that the "writer" he had to talk with was affectionately known as "Dad," à la "Poppa" Hemingway, Peggy greets the open-mouthed Harry by that title, as she announces that she must go to the liquor store for the Grand Marnier, and leaves again, completely oblivious to the havoc her appearance has caused. Now the injured and infuriated father is about to leave this den of iniquity, convinced that even his docile twenty-one year old has become a "bum," when he is intercepted by the entrance of a somewhat ruffled Alan. Once more, the playwright uses the telephone as an instrument of plot complication, with Harry slowing down his exit to eavesdrop on Alan's conversation. It is Mr. Meltzer, and it becomes obvious at once from Alan's behavior that Mrs. Meltzer and a "French" girl had arrived at the Hotel Croyden suite simultaneously (a result of Mrs. Baker's inept message-taking in the previous scene), so that the infuriated Meltzer is considering a "lawsuit." That word activates Harry Baker, who takes over, confirms his suspicion that it was Alan who had arranged for the "party" and then stalks to the door of the apartment in ominous silence, turning only to utter a very strange benediction as he leaves. He says:

May you and your brother live and be well. God bless you, all
the luck in the world, you should know nothing but happiness.
If I ever speak to either one of you again, my tongue should fall
out.

After Mr. Baker has made his exit, the brothers are alone for
only a few minutes, when Connie arrives, bag and baggage in
hand. She is ready to move in, but Alan suffers a complete
regression to his family's standards of behavior. As he says,
"Look, I told you before. I'm not denying anything. Six nights a
week I'm Leonard Lover. But with you—well, you're different."
He admits that he loves her, but uses the excuse that he's just
lost his job—so they can't get married right now. By the time he
is ready to "surrender," Connie asserts, "I don't take
prisoners. . . . If that's the way you'll marry me, I don't want
it." She is ready to leave and is so angry that she refuses to
believe that it is Alan's mother now calling her son to tell him
that his father will be sleeping at Aunt Gussie's. Since Alan is
very upset, his mood matches his mother's, and he promises to
return to his old boyhood room at least for the night. The curtain
goes down as Mrs. Baker is obviously asking Alan what he
wants for supper. A concerned mother to the bitter end.

Act III takes place after a three week time lapse, during
which the two brothers have really exchanged personalities.
Buddy is gay, carefree, completely confident; Alan is worried,
depressed, totally dejected. Now it is Buddy who is trying to
cheer Alan; it is Buddy who cannot go to a movie with his
brother because he has a date; and it is Buddy who fearlessly
opens the door to Peggy, playing Mr. Manheim without a
qualm. He brushes her off because he has to "look at some
locations," and she turns to Alan, who is totally uninterested in
another skiing week-end. All through this scene Buddy does
everything which Alan did in Act I, but he overdoes it, so that he
aggravates Alan and amuses the audience simultaneously.
Finally, he suggests that his brother stay out until one o'clock
because this may be the night to "conquer Mt. Everest," since
his latest girl's name is Snow. At this final affront, Alan
explodes:

BUDDY: You don't mind going to a movie, do you?
ALAN: You're damned right I mind!
BUDDY: What's wrong, Alan? That was our arrangement,
        wasn't it? If one fellow had a girl—
ALAN: That was MY arrangement. I did the arranging and
        YOU went to the movies. Where do you get this OUR
        stuff?
BUDDY: I thought we were splitting everything fifty-fifty.
ALAN: We were until you got all the fifties.

The bickering continues, until Alan finally stoops to telling
Buddy to stay away from his Fig Newtons, to which Buddy
answers kiddingly, "I don't understand. I always give you some
of my Yankee Doodles." And at this moment it is clear that Alan
has become a younger version of Harry Baker. He even calls
Buddy a bum, and becomes as illogical as his father when he
defends his own swinging behavior by saying, "We're not
talking about a thirty-three-year-old-bum. We're talking about
a twenty-one-year-old-bum." They continue to argue with Alan
becoming less and less reasonable until finally, he threatens to
slap Buddy across the face and Buddy says he is going to move
out.

    At this moment Mama returns to the apartment, this time
lugging a suitcase. She explains that for the past three weeks
Harry has been even nastier than usual, and today, on their
thirty-seventh wedding anniversary, he had been particularly
verbal about "her two bums." Again, the doorbell interrupts
the "scene," and as Mrs. Baker drags her valise into the
bedroom, because the visitor is expected to be Buddy's date,
Snow, Harry Baker appears to claim "their mother." His use of
the third person adds to the comic effect as he says, "I thought
I'd find *her* in here. *She* should be home. I'm still *her*
husband." He reveals that he has tickets in his pocket for a
four-month trip around the world and that he intends to sell the
waxed fruit business. Mrs. Baker asserts that she is not "going
around any worlds" until all is right with their sons, and even
her husband's threat to take his sister, Gussie, in her place
doesn't move her. Once more the doorbell rings, and we get a
quasi-vaudeville bit when Connie comes in to say she's just

returned from Cincinnati, where she had been "Miss Automatic Toaster." She will now accept the Electrical Dealers' offer to go to Europe, all expenses paid. Since Mr. Baker assumes that she is the kind of girl he's run into at Alan's earlier, he misinterprets everything she says. Now it is the telephone which interrupts the marriage proposal scene taking place between Alan and Connie, but since it is a long sought-after customer with a large order for waxed fruit (engineered on the sly by the repentant Alan), all is well. The now-betrothed couple and the elder Bakers agree to go out to dinner together after Alan has admitted that his father had been right about many things all along. He *had* been a BUM! Their exit leaves Buddy on stage alone, awaiting Snow and an exciting evening, but the doorbell rings for the last time to reveal Aunt Gussie, who has "just dropped in to say hello."

There is little doubt that from this slick first-effort by Neil Simon it would be difficult to predict that this playwright would develop into the major figure he has become. The craftsmanship is there, despite the over-reliance on the doorbell and telephone; the ability to write very funny dialogue is there; even the seed of thematic importance is there. What is lacking is the later consistency in characterization which gives verisimilitude and universality to so much of his work. Nevertheless, what is patently obvious is that while the playwright's vision has broadened and deepened, the critics, on the whole, have persisted in viewing all his subsequent plays as though they were merely frothy variations of *Come Blow Your Horn*. This notion is simply untrue.

1. There is an interesting parallel between Alan's "giving" Buddy this girl as a birthday gift and Neil Simon's use of the same kind of gift in "Visitor from Philadelphia," the second playlet in *California Suite*, written fifteen years later.

2. Felix Ungar becomes one of the protagonists in *The Odd Couple*, written four years after *Come Blow Your Horn*, but he is obviously an entirely different character from the drama coach mentioned by Peggy. Only the name is the same.

Barefoot in the Park

First presented at the Biltmore Theatre, New York City, by Saint Subber, October 23, 1963.

Director: Mike Nichols

Setting: Oliver Smith

Lighting: Jean Rosenthal

Costumes: Donald Brooks

CAST

Corie Bratter	Elizabeth Ashley
Telephone Repair Man	Herbert Edelman
Delivery Man	Joseph Keating
Paul Bratter	Robert Redford
Corie's Mother, Mrs. Banks	Mildred Natwick
Victor Velasco	Kurt Kaznar

Number of Performances: 1,530

Barefoot In The Park — Photo by Joseph Abeles Studio
(Actors, left to right) Mildred Natwick, Elizabeth Ashley,
Kurt Kaznar, Robert Redford

Barefoot in the Park (1963)

Neil Simon's second play, a simple comedy plotwise, is quite different in style from his first. For one thing, there are some ridiculous situations, but they are much less contrived and stem almost entirely from characterization. Furthermore, there is little use made of "the running gag," such as the doorbell and telephone in *Come Blow Your Horn*. Even more significantly, the characters are more believable, better motivated, and much farther from "stock" types than those in Simon's first play. Finally, there are definite philosophical viewpoints expressed— comments about the ways life can and should be lived. It is quite frankly a romantic comedy, and if Neil Simon had gone no farther, it would certainly be an impertinence to compare his works with those of playwrights who have used the comic mode to make serious statements on a universal level. The point, however, is that he has traveled a long way from the park, along an ever-widening and ever-deepening path, a circumstance which should become evident as each of his plays is considered in turn.

As the curtain rises, Corie Bratter, a radiant young newlywed, opens the door of her first apartment, and her pleasant, optimistic nature is immediately conveyed to the audience by the way she surveys the drab empty room with rapture. It is February, but Corie has brought a bunch of flowers with her, and we just know at once that this vacant space will be transformed in short order to a tasteful lovenest, secure against casual intrusion from the outside world since it is the top floor of an old reconverted brownstone, five flights (six if you count the front stoop) above New York's teeming streets. Almost immediately, the telephone installer pants his way into paradise, followed closely by a Lord and Taylor delivery "boy" of about sixty who never manages to speak at all because of

having barely completed the climb. Then Paul, Corie's proper
young lawyer-husband, negotiates the stairs, surprised at how
many flights he must climb, as he had seen only the third-floor
version before renting. Finally, Ethel Banks, Corie's mother,
"drops in" on her way from a luncheon in Westchester to her
home in New Jersey.

At this point, the expected furniture delivery has still not
materialized, but Corie's mother hastens to reassure the young
bride that she can imagine how perfect the place will be after
Corie has worked on it. When Paul goes down five (six) flights
to get some Scotch, Ethel states a major theme of the play and
defines character as well, as she and Corie continue to discuss
the apartment. The mother says, "Well it is unusual—like you.
. . . What about Paul? I worry about you two. You're so
impulsive. You jump into life. Paul is like me; he looks first." At
this stage we also get a picture of Ethel as a lovely but lonely
widow who lives by herself way out in New Jersey, but who
obviously has not considered alternative life-styles which might
include traveling, a job, or love in the sexual sense. Apparently,
Corie is her main interest.

Just as Paul returns with the liquor, an unseen Aunt Harriet
rings the bell to call for Ethel, who leaves, promising to return
on Friday for the "official unveiling." Paul then sets the scene
for the entrance of the fourth major character in the play. It
seems that a conversation with the liquor store clerk has
revealed that the Bratters have "some of the greatest weirdos in
the country" right in their building, one of whom is known as
"The Bluebeard of 48th Street," or Victor Velasco. Since there
is a hole in the skylight which is causing a draft, and since Paul
is much more concerned with preparing for his first case in court
than with Corie's romantic plans for the evening, he decides to
go into the bedroom to stand and work (they have no chairs!),
leaving Corie alone to greet the 58-year-old pixie who comes to
the door to request permission to crawl through the Bratters'
window to reach his apartment. It seems that this is Victor and
that he's been locked out of his attic apartment because he's
four months behind in his rent. He takes everything very
lightly, and invites himself, charmingly, of course, for dinner on
Friday night. Then, after meeting Paul briefly, he exits into the

bedroom, making his last appearance as he crawls across the skylight. Paul is stunned, not only by seeing Victor in this precarious position, but also at Corie's phone call to her mother, reconfirming Friday evening's plans. The curtain falls as Victor waves cheerfully at the newlyweds.

As Act II, scene 1, opens, the audience sees the almost miraculous changes accomplished by the imaginative decorating skills of the bride, aided peripherally we learn by the intrepid Victor, who had "helped" by ordering Paul to move furniture around until 3 a.m. Friday morning. The young attorney has won his first case, but since his client had only been awarded six cents as "protection of his good name," it can hardly be classed an outstanding victory. Furthermore, Paul is annoyed at his wife for arranging a "blind date" for her mother, especially when he finds out that Mrs. Banks had been told that the other guests would be Paul's parents, rather than Victor Velasco. In short, the young husband is hardly in a party mood, and he is almost rude when the "Count of Monte Cristo" arrives sans wine (which he didn't have the money to buy), but with an epicurean delight known as knichi as a substitute. It is imperative, he announces, that the knichis must be "popped" into the mouth to be fully appreciated, a feat managed only by Corie. Actually, as the cocktails and small talk continue, we see clearly that it is only she who enters into the spirit of the evening, which is precisely what we would expect of the character. Finally, the two couples set out for an "adventure in dining" at an Albanian restaurant on Staten Island, suggested by Victor. Mrs. Banks, by this time half drunk from Corie's martinis (made earlier with *equal* parts of gin and vermouth), plus a belt of Paul's Scotch, stoutly asserts that she is "one of the fellows," so it is Paul who is most obviously annoyed by the gaiety of the others.

It is simple to imagine what has happened during the interim, as Corie and Victor return to the Bratters' apartment at the beginning of scene 2, breathless and laughing, prepared to continue the party with coffee or brandy and an old Albanian folk song, *Shama, Shama,* although it is now 2 a.m. In sharp contrast, Paul follows, literally carrying the almost unconscious Mrs. Banks, who announces almost at once that she must now return to New Jersey. Victor, "the complete gentleman," insists on taking her home, even though the buses back to New York have already stopped running for the night. As he exits, he says, "If you don't hear from us in a week, we'll be at the Nacional Hotel in Mexico City—Room 703," a remark which triggers a really serious argument between Paul and Corie. Of course, they are both somewhat drunk; nevertheless, Simon makes their divergent views of life as delineated earlier by Mrs. Banks, crystal clear. Paul accuses his wife of being unconcerned about her mother, and she answers:

> Unconcerned. . . I'm plenty concerned. Do you think I'm going to get one wink of sleep until that phone rings tomorrow? I'm scared to death for my mother. But I'm grateful there's finally the opportunity for something to be scared about. What I'm really concerned about is you! I'm beginning to wonder if you're capable of having a good time.

She goes on to tell him that he has no sense of adventure, that he's a Watcher, not a Do-er, and finally, that he's "extremely proper and dignified," if not a stuffed shirt! Paul retaliates by attempting to hold on to his emotions and go to sleep without getting into a real knock-down, drag-out battle, a reaction which infuriates Corie. She reminds him that he would not walk with her "barefoot in the park" the other night, and he reminds her that it was 17 degrees. As the verbal exchange continues, Paul tries to keep his temper, but Corie keeps baiting him and finally tells him that she wants a divorce. There is an amusing bit of "shtick" about which person will spend the night in the bedroom, but Paul is outmaneuvered, and tries to settle down to sleep on the couch with Corie crying loudly in the bedroom in an attempt to keep him awake all night. Now the phone rings, and a furious Paul in a misplaced-object temper tantrum rips the instrument from the wall and tries to go to sleep as the snow from the hole in the skylight falls on his exposed head. Curtain.

Act III finds the alienated lovers taking oblique shots at one another as the telephone man from the first scene is trying to fix the telephone and remain outside the line of fire at the same time. There are some very humorous moments as Paul takes his "dinner" of grapes from his attaché case after refusing Corie's goulash, and then tries to snatch some of the hot food from her plate when she is behind the kitchen screen. Paul has not had time to look for his own place yet; Corie pretends an advertisement for dancing lessons is a personal call; and on and on, until at last there is a call from Aunt Harriet informing Corie that her mother's bed has not been slept in, and that the good lady is missing! At this point Corie rushes out to find Victor, while Paul continues to pack his things, but before he actually leaves the apartment, Corie returns obviously very disturbed. Paul thinks of an accident and rushes to comfort Corie just as Ethel Banks comes in, very disheveled and dressed only in a large man's bathrobe and slippers. Both of the young people believe the worst of Corie's mother, so that when Paul leaves, Corie voices her realization that he was "right all along." Ethel, now quite distraught at the thought of what her daughter and son-in-law must think of her, explains the situation in humorous terms. She says:

> When I got outside I suddenly felt dizzy . . . and I fainted. Well, I passed out . . . in the slush. Then Victor picked me up and carried me inside. I couldn't walk because my shoes fell down the sewer. He started to carry me up here but his beret fell over his eyes and he fell down the stairs. He fell into Apartment 3C. I fell on his foot. . . . They had to carry us up. Mr. Gonzales, Mr. Armandariz and Mr. Calhoun. They carried us up. . . And then they put us down. On the rugs. Oh, he doesn't have beds, just thick rugs. And then I fell asleep. And then when I woke up, Victor was gone. But I was there . . . in his bathrobe. I swear that's the truth, Corie.

Of course, the girl wants to know what happened to her mother's clothes and can hardly be blamed for not believing that Mrs. Banks does not know. At this point the playwright begins the denouement, as Victor enters to clear up the mystery of the missing clothes (which are at the cleaners), at the same time admitting that his toe is broken and that he has ulcers, so that he must take the same little pink pills that Ethel takes. Furthermore, he dyes his hair! As he invites Mrs. Banks to a *plain* dinner that evening, she realizes that for the first time in years she has slept without the board which she had always required for her ailing back and is celebrating by popping a grape into her mouth, à la knichi, when she becomes aware of Corie, now tearful about her own problems with Paul. Ethel then gives her daughter advice which carries a somewhat chauvinistic message. She says:

> You've just got to give up a little of you for him. Take care of him. And make him feel important. And if you can do that, you'll have a happy and wonderful marriage.

But Neil Simon redeems himself a bit with the next line, "Like two out of every ten couples."

In any case, after her mother's joyful exit—presumably to go to a new life style which will include the now chastened Victor—Corie starts to go out to hunt for her missing husband. As she opens the door, however, there he stands—very drunk and burning up with fever because he's been walking "barefoot in the park," despite having a heavy cold. Paul now announces a solution for their problem: he wants Corie to move out since he's the one paying the rent. As he becomes more and more obnoxious, Corie barricades herself in the bathroom and decides she wants the "old Paul" back. Again, her speech would not be pleasing to women libbers, as she defends her husband's original personality:

> He's not a fuddy duddy. He's dependable and he's strong and he takes care of me and tells me how much I can spend and protects me from people like you. [the "new" Paul] And I just want him to know how much I love him, and that I'm going to fix the hole in the skylight and the leak in the closet . . . and I'm going to put in a bathtub and if he wants, I'll even carry him up the stairs every night. . .

When she gets no audible response, Corie finally emerges to find that her husband has climbed up onto the skylight and is in great peril of falling, drunk as he is, off the roof. Corie is quite prepared to go out and pull him in and tells him to sing until she gets to him since he is now thoroughly unnerved. This he does, but the only song he can remember is the hated *Shama, Shama,* the Albanian folk song which had so aggravated him the night before! The curtain falls on this happy ending.

Quite obviously the young Bratters represent two diverse philosophies: two ways of dealing with life. Corie leaps effortlessly into Victor Velasco's hedonistic approach, whereas Paul "looks first," holds back, and frequently never jumps at all. Ethel Banks, of course, starts out a conservative (in the correct sense of that word) like her son-in-law, but she undergoes some rather abrupt changes, along with the "Bluebeard of 48th Street" who ends by allowing his beard to "go gray." In a very real sense each of the four characters has altered his behavior so that it has become less polarized, less radical, less extreme. Each person has gravitated toward a moderation which seems to be the playwright's ideal. Back in Act II when Paul envisions the meeting of Corie's mother and Victor as an unmitigated fiasco, he says, "You saw his apartment. He wears Japanese kimonos and sleeps on rugs. Your mother wears a hair net and sleeps on a board." By the end of the play, however, it is clear that Paul has overlooked Ethel's secret desire for flamboyance, just as he has misunderstood his romantic wife, Corie, who wants to live as though all of life were a honeymoon. His walking "barefoot in the park" is his concession to non-conformity, then, just as Corie's final speech about the "old Paul" signifies her admission that she must accept a more conventional relationship since her young husband must spend some of his time working to support them. Paul, we feel, will think twice before assuming the role of "stuffed shirt" again; Corie will become a bit more cautious in her behavior. And all will be well—the proper ending for this pleasant comedy.

It is interesting that Neil Simon has made a point here regarding the desirability of following a middle course in order to live pleasurably without boredom, but with a sensible regard for responsibility. Such a stand against extremism is reminiscent of Molière and Jonson both, thematically speaking, and it is clearly important to him, since in his next play, *The Odd Couple,* he deals even more cogently with the matter. As we shall see, next time the two characters representing incompatible philosophies actually do get the "divorce" which

Corie and Paul do not really want nor need, showing even more forcibly that unless some compromise is effected, some middle ground agreed upon, it is impossible for human beings to live in harmony, each clinging tenaciously to a view of life which allows for no other.

The Odd Couple

First presented at the Plymouth Theatre, New York City, by Saint Subber, March 10, 1965.

Director: Mike Nichols

Setting: Oliver Smith

Lighting: Jean Rosenthal

Costumes: Ann Roth

CAST

Speed	Paul Donley
Murray	Nathaniel Frey
Roy	Sidney Armus
Vinnie	John Fiedler
Oscar Madison	Walter Matthau
Felix Ungar	Art Carney
Gwendolyn Pigeon	Carole Shelley
Cecily Pigeon	Monica Evans

Number of Performances: 964

The Odd Couple — Photo by Joseph Abeles Studio
(Actors, left to right) Walter Matthau, Art Carney

The Odd Couple (1965)

In this play Neil Simon has captured the essence of incompatibility among humans who repeat again and again their self-defeating patterns of personality, patterns which make it impossible for them to live together, all good intentions notwithstanding. It really does not matter that the two main characters, Oscar Madison and Felix Ungar (no connection to the unseen drama coach of the same name mentioned in *Come Blow Your Horn*), are both men. They could be women, or they could be a married couple in the traditional sense. What does matter is that the playwright is making a very humorous statement to the effect that although opposites may attract, they also exasperate, frequently to the point that the only viable alternative to murder is divorce. Even more noteworthy is the fact that the playwright has begun to allow his characters free rein in earnest, and he has been forced by them to do what amounts to an almost about-face in regard to sexual stereotyping.

In his first two plays Neil Simon appeared, albeit unconsciously, to be a strict traditionalist in regard to men and women: their roles, their expectations, their behavior. In *The Odd Couple,* however, although there is some exaggeration to heighten the comedy, Simon is obliged by his characters to present them as men with totally different orientations to life, not at all connected to their masculinity or lack thereof. For example, in the stage directions which precede Act I, Oscar's apartment is described as follows:

> *Although the furnishings have been chosen with extreme good taste, the room itself, without the TOUCH AND CARE OF A WOMAN these past few months, is now a study in slovenliness.*

But very soon it is Felix's "touch and care"—and he is very much a man—which makes it impossible for Oscar to live with him. In much the same way, it is apparent early in the play that it is Frances, Felix's wife, who has demanded their separation and is still totally in charge of the situation. Nevertheless, Felix voices the cliché:

> It's so much harder on the woman, Oscar. She's all alone with the kids. Stuck there in the house. She can't get out like me. I mean, where is she going to find someone now at her age? With two kids? Where?

The statement gets a well-deserved laugh from the audience, since it is patently obvious that it is *he* who can't "make it alone." Throughout the play, without resorting to the kind of gimmick used many years ago by George S. Kaufman, in his one-act-play "If Men Played Cards as Women Do," in which men simply parrot typical "girl-talk," Simon presents his characters realistically and lets the laughs come where they will when it becomes apparent that males when placed in certain situations behave in ways popularly if incorrectly labeled "feminine."

Act I opens on the only "running gag" in the play—a weekly poker game, repeated in Acts II and III, each planned to show the relationship which exists between the two major characters. Because the playwright is skilled at creating people recognizable to his audience, the minor poker players come off as distinct individuals who interact humorously just because they are what they are, rather than by reason of one-liners. There is Murray, the policeman, a good-natured clod, who will never become a crack detective. There is Roy, Oscar Madison's accountant, somewhat sarcastic about the unpleasant odors of dirt in the first act, but equally put out by the smell of ammonia in Act II. There is Vinnie, who is going to Florida in the middle of summer because the rates are cheapest then, the winner who must "leave early," a definite cheapskate. And there is Speed, who is interested primarily in playing cards with his male friends in order to "get away from the aggravation" he has at home. The main characters, Oscar Madison and Felix Ungar, complete the "card club."

As the curtain rises, only five of the men are present in Oscar's apartment, growling and grousing about everything from the hot weather to the poor refreshments. This is undoubtedly not a new scenario for these friends, but they are more out of sorts than usual because the sixth player, Felix, who hasn't missed a game in over two years, is unusually late. We get a good preview of this unseen character from the discussion about what circumstances could account for his absence when Murray says:

> Hey, maybe he's in his office locked in the john again. Did you know Felix was once locked in the john overnight? He wrote out his entire will on a half a roll of toilet paper.

We also get a full-blown picture of Oscar as a very careless and supposedly carefree person as he good-naturedly continues to borrow money from the other players to "stay in the game," and laughingly describes the brown and green sandwiches as "either very new cheese or very old meat." He is also far behind in his alimony and child support payments for his ex-wife, Blanche, who now lives in California, but this debt doesn't seem to disturb him either. When Roy suggests that he could be jailed for non-support of his children, Oscar says, "Never. If she can't call me once a week to aggravate me, she's not happy." Finally, all of the conjecture about Felix's whereabouts comes to an end as Murray's wife calls to say she has just talked to Frances Ungar and learned that Felix is "missing." What Oscar learns when he checks with Frances is that the Ungars have split up—permanently—and it soon becomes very clear that it is Frances who could no longer stand the marriage. Therefore, Felix has gone out to kill himself, taking care, however, to send his wife a "suicide telegram" as a precautionary measure.

From this moment until the appearance of a disheveled Felix, shortly thereafter, we learn that this man is "a nut," a hypochondriac, a crybaby, and, in short, a compulsive hysteric, to borrow a term from popular psychology. Nevertheless, the other men are genuinely concerned about his welfare, although they try to mask their feelings (in a supposedly macho fashion) by pretending complete absorption in their poker game when he arrives. After some very funny shenanigans perpetrated to try to prevent Felix's suicide, Oscar finally gets rid of the other four men and tries to deal with him on a one-to-one basis. During this interchange we begin to see under the stereotyped conformities two rather nice human beings who will never be able to communicate with one another simply because each man has a completely different way of viewing the world and is committed to what amounts to an extreme position with no intention of compromise. Felix admits, "It's a lousy marriage, but I still love her. . . . We didn't get along. But we had two wonderful kids and a beautiful home." And continues, "What more does she want? What does any woman want?" without understanding (then *or* later in his relationship to Oscar) that what any human being wants and needs in a "marriage" is an ability to glide gracefully to middle ground. Oscar calls him "the only man in the world with clenched hair," in the same way as Frances had told him that his tombstone would read, "Here *stands* Felix Ungar," and this inflexibility will continue to block his achieving happiness regardless of the sex of the "mate" he chooses.

Underlying his behavior is Felix's feeling that he is "nothing" without Frances and the children—that he doesn't want to change his life. This is a common problem with people who define themselves in terms of their jobs, their families—in short, in terms of extraneous circumstances and/or other people. Oscar, on the other hand, who is just as "lost" without his family, has a healthier ego. He admonishes Felix and one feels that he has come to terms with himself when he says:

> What do you mean, nothing! You're something! A person! You're flesh and bones and hair and nails and ears. You're not a fish. You're not a buffalo. You're *you!*

Felix is all too ready to admit his peculiarities, but he does it in the manner of an alcoholic who recognizes his failing, but takes just one more drink to help him make the climb onto the wagon. He is powerless to change. For instance, he says:

You don't know what I was like at home. I bought her a book
and made her write down every penny we spent. And then we
had a big fight because I said she forgot to write down how
much the book was.

When Oscar tries to comfort him with, "We all have faults,"
Felix continues:

Faults? . . . We have a maid who comes in to clean three times a
week. And on the other days, Frances does the cleaning. And at
night, after they've both cleaned up, I go in and clean the whole
place again. I loused up the marriage. Nothing was ever right. I
used to recook everything. The minute she walked out of the
kitchen, I would add salt or pepper. It's not that I didn't trust
her; it's just that I was a better cook.

He then asserts that he hates himself and is genuinely surprised
at Oscar's more accurate assessment that he really loves
himself, which, of course, he does in the sense that he thinks his
way is always the only right way, a conviction which evokes
inevitable conflict and causes him to fail in his relationships
with other people.

When Oscar proposes a solution, that Felix share his apartment, we get a glimpse of the "carefree" man's genuine feeling
as he gruffly points out that he'd rather live with Felix, who he
agrees is a "pest," than continue to live alone. Frances Ungar
telephones in the midst of their conversation, but only to say
that she wants Felix to come and get his things so that she can
have the room repainted. Naturally, this idea is very amusing,
and is something of an exaggeration for the sake of provoking
audience laughter; however, her suggestion does serve to
expose Felix even more fully, as now realizing that his marriage
is over, he decides to "rearrange his life," requesting a pencil
and paper, presumably to list the specific changes! Further, he
promises not to do too much cleaning up before he turns in—
just the dishes—and when Oscar retires, Felix, busily plumping
up the couch pillows, says, "Good night, Frances," completely
unaware of his error.

Act II, scene 1, takes place two weeks later, and as the

audience expects, Oscar's apartment is now not just clean, but "spotless and sterile," to use the playwright's description. Felix is serving the poker players their refreshments, and, without any burlesquing of female mannerisms, is giving the impression of a proud if somewhat finicky hostess carefully serving drinks and food to admiring guests. Oscar is sarcastic about "rings left on the table when coasters are not placed under the glasses," and Speed and Roy take the same stance. Vinnie and Murray, however, are enjoying the tasty food and the attentive service. After the guests leave, we find that all is not well in this paradise. Felix has been playing "Mr. Clean," as Oscar puts it, and making Oscar feel guilty about such activities as walking on the floors. Furthermore, Felix won't fight; he only pouts and sulks and then makes matters worse by "giving in" to every criticism of his irritating habits. Felix threatens to throw a cup, but reconsiders, so Oscar tries to sell him the idea of letting loose once in his life:

> You do something you *feel* like doing—and not what you *think* you're supposed to do. Stop keeping books. Felix. Relax. Get drunk. Get angry. C'mon, break the goddamed cup!

Finally, he gets through; Felix does hurl the cup, but his action results only in a hurt arm, at which Oscar appears to give up. He does make one more stab at getting his friend to behave more normally with the suggestion that they "double date" with two women who live in the apartment building—the Pigeon sisters. When Felix ultimately agrees, there is some ominous fore-shadowing of the way the evening will go as the scene closes with Felix telephoning Frances for her London broil recipe. He will cook the dinner!

Scene 2 is pure plagiarism, if one is willing to define that term broadly. Anyone who has gone through the dialogue with a late-arriving husband cannot help but think that Neil Simon must have had a hidden microphone on the scene and simply transcribed the conversation. It is eight o'clock; Oscar was to be home at seven. He hadn't called because he'd stopped in Hannigan's Bar for a drink on the way; the London broil is overdone; and the guests have not made their appearance.

Oscar's reaction to Felix's "silent treatment" is so typical that it is side-splitting. And when the "injured party" finally talks, he emphasizes every word by waving a ladle in Oscar's face. In the midst of a discussion about gravy, the ladies (appropriately called the Pigeon sisters—"Not spelled like Walter Pidgeon, but like Coo-Coo pigeon," as Gwendolyn explains) come to the door. These two are not very realistically drawn, but they need not be; they are interchangeable characters in the same way that Shakespeare made Rosencrantz and Guildenstern (in *Hamlet*) interchangeable; they exist for plot alone. At any rate, after some awkward introductions, Oscar exits to the kitchen to make the drinks, leaving Felix alone with the two "birds."[1] At first, he's clumsy at small-talk, but soon Felix manages to confess that although Oscar is divorced, he is only separated. He then goes on to expound at length on the "inhumanity of divorce" and quite quickly gets around to showing the girls pictures of Frances, his children, even his living room! In a very few minutes Oscar returns to find that the Pigeons have joined Felix in having a good cry, and the whole party has turned into a wake. The sisters think it is a "rare quality in a man to be able to cry," and they're not too far off, except that Felix's tears are really shed in self-pity, as much for his charred London broil as for his lost family. In any case, the dinner is ruined, so the Pigeons invite the two men to their apartment for "pot luck," a suggestion which strikes Oscar as just dandy. As he puts it, "Do you know what's waiting for us up there? You've just been invited to spend the evening in a two-bedroom hothouse with the Coo-Coo Pigeon sisters!" Felix, however, decides that he won't go and nothing Oscar says can change his mind. He states flatly that he has used up all his conversation and that he's going to scrub pots and wash his hair, a plan which infuriates his room-mate. The act ends as Oscar says, "You mean you're not going to make any effort to change? This is the person you're going to be—until the day you die?" and becomes so incensed by Felix's "We are what we are," that he opens the window wide and pulls back the drapes in a comical pantomimed invitation to Felix to jump.

The pre-poker game preparations (Felix vacuuming the rug and tidying up) open the final act. But the events of the night before have changed Oscar from a nettled gnat to a raging bull. He deliberately taunts Felix, and since the two men are not speaking, the laughs here depend on the excellence in timing mimetic actions. In desperation, Oscar offers Felix an ultimatum: if he wishes to continue living in this apartment, he must stay in his room. Naturally, the indignant Felix asserts his rights—he pays half the rent—and the fight takes off from there. In a genuine fit of fury Oscar hurls Felix's plate of food across the living room, aiming for the kitchen wall. He says the spaghetti is now garbage, which only brings a titter from Felix who informs him that it's linguini, not spaghetti. Ultimately, in desperation, Oscar tells his friend that he cannot stand his behavior any longer. He says:

> For six months I lived alone in this apartment. All alone in eight rooms. I was dejected, despondent and disgusted. Then you moved in—my dearest and closest friend. And after three months of close, personal contact—I am about to have a nervous breakdown! Do me a favor. Move into the kitchen. Live with your pots, your pans, your ladle and your meat thermometer. When you want to come out, ring a bell and I'll run into the bedroom. I'm asking you nicely, Felix, as a friend. Stay out of my way!

He then exits into the bedroom, but Felix calls after him, "Walk on the paper, will you? The floors are wet," which proves the proverbial straw to the camel's back. Oscar returns ready to settle his problem with Felix physically, but thinks of an even more efficacious solution before he strikes a blow. He goes to Felix's room and returns with a suitcase. Felix still does not comprehend what is being suggested until Oscar tells him in no uncertain terms that "the whole marriage is over," and that he wants his room-mate to pack up and move out that very night.

Finally understanding that Oscar is completely serious, Felix still insists on having the final words. "Fine," he says, "but remember what happens to me is your responsibility. Let it be on your head." Oscar takes all this quite seriously—not the curse really—but the way Felix is behaving, and he counters with, "Felix, we've been friends a long time. For the sake of that friendship, please say, 'Oscar, we can't stand each other;

let's break up.'" Completely in character, Felix will have none
of such a reasonable attitude. He prefers to imply by his words
and his behavior that he will now commit suicide and that it will
be Oscar's fault. After he has left the apartment with "that
human sacrifice" look on his face again, an obviously upset host
greets the other poker players and admits that he has thrown
Felix out, trying at the same time to justify his behavior. Murray
counters with, "We all know he's impossible, but he's still our
friend, and he's still out on the street, and I'm still worried
about him." Anything but a hard-boiled "masculine" reaction
typical of a New York City policeman, but again entirely logical
for this character. Oscar then voices his guilt feelings: "I'm
not worried? Who do you think sent him out there in the first
place?" which triggers a very perceptive comment as Murray
replies:

> Frances sent him out in the first place. You sent him out in the
> second place. And whoever he lives with next will send him out
> in the third place. Don't you understand? It's Felix. He does it
> to himself. I don't know why. He doesn't know why. There are
> people like that.

Oscar does understand; nevertheless, he is very concerned
about Felix and is only too happy to hear the doorbell. At this
sound, the poker players repeat their behavior of Act I—pretending to play cards and act unconcerned—but this time it is
not a distraught Felix at the door; it's Gwendolyn Pigeon. She
has come for Felix's things and her description of him as a
"sweet tortured man" is really too much for Oscar to accept. At
this moment, sister Cecily Pigeon comes in, dragging a
reluctant Felix with her. He has told the girls that he "really
doesn't want to stay with them," so Cecily has come to get
Gwendolyn to help her persuade the "poor man." A supposedly
unwilling Felix finally agrees to stay with the Pigeons for a few
days "until he finds his own place," and the good ladies then
exit to prepare dinner for him.

The other poker players stare dumbfounded as Felix comes
out of the bedroom carrying two suits in a plastic cleaner's bag
and starts toward the door, but the pragmatic Oscar is still

worrying about Felix's curse: "Remember what happens to me is your responsibility. Let it be on your head." Perhaps he suspects that the Pigeons will soon toss him out of their nest, starting him on the road to suicide once more. In any case, he stops Felix to ask jokingly, "Aren't you going to thank me?. . . for the two greatest things I ever did for you. Taking you in and throwing you out." And Felix generously replies, ". . . In gratitude, I remove the curse." As if in jest, Oscar says, "Oh, bless and thank you, Wicked Witch of the North," and the two men shake hands remaining friends as many divorced heterosexual couples do. Oscar's ex-wife then calls long distance and that conversation also seems to contrast with its earlier parallel in Act I, so the audience may assume that they are "friends" again too. What the playwright is saying is that all can be well between couples, as long as those who don't belong together don't try to live in an impossible proximity. And the poker game continues as the curtain comes down.

Neil Simon has publicly stated that many women have identified with Oscar and Felix and their situation, a fact which should not be surprising. As characters in *The Odd Couple* these two men are all too close to reality; they are not manipulated by the playwright, but actually represent scores of individuals of both sexes who can accomodate one another even in a long-lasting friendship, but who find it virtually impossible to parlay that friendship into an even closer relationship— marriage and the daily living which that entails. It is not that Felix is compulsively neat whereas Oscar is careless; it is not that Felix cries aloud while Oscar represses his feelings; it is not even that their total "chemistries" clash when they are forced to see each other on a daily basis. More significantly, neither man is able to compromise, particularly Felix, on even the smallest details of living. This kind of insensitivity to the need for mutual concession may be the genuine "grounds for divorce," rather than money or in-law trouble, statistics notwithstanding. Furthermore, what both men lack, and again, especially Felix, is a sense of humor, the variety which enables both men and women to see their own peculiarities and laugh, accepting themselves as parts played in the human comedy.

As always, Neil Simon's view is a benign one, tempered no

doubt by his own warm and sympathetic attitude toward even the less attractive specimens of humanity. It is clear, however, that in this play he begins in earnest to deal in the comic genre with an ongoing and universal concern: the inevitable need for a middle course rather than an extremely polarized position in pursuit of harmony, if not ecstasy. And these two people would need to recognize this requirement were they both women or a heterosexual couple. In this sense, the playwright has significantly altered his previously held position regarding innate sexual differences, a position which he was probably quite unaware of having before creating *The Odd Couple*.

1. This is a rather subtle joke, as the Pigeons are English and the slang word for "broads" or "dames" in Cockney parlance is "birds."

The Star Spangled Girl — Photo by Joseph Abeles Studio
(Actors, left to right) Connie Stevens, Richard Benjamin,
Anthony Perkins

The Star Spangled Girl

First presented at the Plymouth Theatre, New York City, by Saint Subber, December 21, 1966.

Director: George Axelrod

Setting: Oliver Smith

Lighting: Jean Rosenthal

Costumes: Ann Roth

CAST

Andy Hobart .... Anthony Perkins
Norman Cornell .... Richard Benjamin
Sophie Rauschmeyer .... Connie Stevens

Number of Performances: 261

The Star Spangled Girl (1966)

There is an interesting idea in this play, but for a number of reasons, it never reaches fruition. First, the three characters who appear in the play are so exaggerated that they belong only in a broad farce, and the playwright never brings on the two additional characters who might complete the joke. Further, the theme of physical attraction versus genuine love becomes blurred, particularly through a contrived denouement which seems necessary only to end the third act, rather than to make any kind of point. Finally, the one-liners, which abound and are quite funny at times, are so obvious that they dominate. In truth, this play can be said to be a step down from its predecessor, *The Odd Couple*, but, fortunately, Neil Simon goes forward from here to *Plaza Suite* and through *California Suite* seldom returns to this level again.

Andy Hobart and Norman Cornell are two high powered, very intelligent and definitely angry young men of the nineteen sixties, dedicated to their underground magazine *Fallout*, which in turn is dedicated to "telling it like it is" about the social and political scene during the troubled decade of the Viet Nam War. At the beginning of the play, their first problem is money, but very early in scene one their second problem, Sophie Rauschmeyer, the star-spangled girl, enters, and from that moment until the end of Act III (and supposedly beyond) she remains the apex of an improbable triangle. Sophie is everything that Andy and Norman are not. She's a provincial from Hunnicut, Arkansas; she a super-patriot of the "America—love it or leave it" variety; she's a female "jock," ashamed of having "failed her country" by coming in fourth in a swimming competition at the Olympics; she has knowledge of the world acquired solely from *The Reader's Digest* and *Sports Illustrated* (which she reads "religiously"); she lacks a sense of humor; and, finally, she's engaged to a Marine sergeant who sounds like a stand-in for John Wayne.

The play opens as Andy comes into a shabby San Francisco duplex which doubles as living quarters and office for the two young men. When he finds Norman away from his desk, he turns on the tape recorder to learn that his partner has been busy eluding a certain Mr. Franklyn, a printer, to whom *Fallout* and company owes $600. This gives the playwright and the actor a chance for some "shtick" right away, as Mr. Franklyn telephones and Andy pretends to be several other people in the game they are playing to avoid a confrontation over the unpaid bill.

At this point neither man is involved with a young girl. Andy is much too busy going out with an old girl, his landlady, Mrs. Mackininee, who sounds like a wonderful zany. She is one of the characters Simon could have put on stage since it would undoubtedly have added fun to the proceedings to see in person the dark-haired widow with the blond braids who avoids middle-aged spread by riding a motorcycle while wearing gold-sequined goggles and a silver lamé jumpsuit, dancing the Watoosie with abandon, riding a surfboard, flying an airplane, and practicing karate. She keeps a firm hold over her young, attractive male companion by not too subtly threatening eviction for non-payment of rent should he refuse her invitations.

Norman is every inch the totally absorbed writer although he does tease about "waiting for a beautiful, gorgeous blonde" to move in next door. Unfortunately, his fantasy becomes reality all too soon, as Sophie R. comes to their door, introduces herself in an outrageous Southern drawl, and gives him a fruitcake from home because "it has rum in it" and she's in training. In addition to her other charms, Sophie "smells good," which becomes pivotal in the complete head-over-heels feeling which Norman experiences and in the play as a whole. He decides at once that he will woo this girl to the exclusion of all other activity, including his work on *Fallout,* and we go to scene 2.

Three days later, Norman, admitting that it's "pure, unadulterated physical attraction," (or as Andy puts it "when one hippopotamus likes another hippopotamus and no questions

asked''), has spent $22.00 on delicacies for a gift basket at the
United Nations Gourmet Shoppe, has painted Sophie's name on
the steps, and has kept track of her every move with the aid of a
telescope trained on the corner where she boards and leaves the
bus. Without a doubt, he has acted like a complete idiot, and all
he's gotten for his pains is a very angry young lady who wants
him to stop bothering her. As she tells him:

> Ah am going to repeat this to you once more and for the last
> time. Ah am ingaged to be married to First Lieutenant Burt
> Fenneman of the United States Marine Corps. And in six weeks
> Ah will be Mrs. First Lieutenant Burt Fenneman of the United
> States Marine Corps. And Ah intend to be happily married to
> him for the rest of mah natural life. Do you understand that?

Norman, of course, does comprehend intellectually, but as
Andy tells him, he has "steam coming out of his ears" over
Sophie, and so he continues to do things for her which she does
not want done. For instance, while she is at work as a swimming
instructor at the YWCA, he insists on mopping her floor
although she has just waxed it, and then knocks her cat into the
toilet while performing this chore. On and on it goes, with Andy
trying to explain to Sophie just what a bright young man
Norman is, albeit Norman is coming close to proving that he is a
lunatic at the same time. Finally, Sophie is dissuaded by Andy
from calling the police, and she also agrees to read an issue of
Fallout. Furthermore, she promises to smile and be polite to the
lovesick Norman in return for Andy's assurances that nothing
more will happen to upset her life. Now to Act II.

Norman has given his word, but he has broken his word in
spades. Not only has he gone to the YWCA in search of Sophie,
but he has visited three times in one week; furthermore, he has
brought her a gift of a duck which has chased and nipped at
everyone. As Sophie tells him, she has been fired without being
given time to "dry off," although she had found a moment to
arrange for Norman's arrest before leaving. Andy then offers
the girl a job with the magazine; the conversation which follows
gives the audience a really good look at her mental capacity. She
says:

> Do you think Ah would work for that bomb aimed at the heart of
> America? Mr. Hobart, Ah don't know if you're a Communist or
> a Fascist, or just a plain old-fashioned traitor, but you are
> certainly no American. . . . All Ah read last night was the Table
> of Contents, but if you don't like the country that gave you your
> birth, why don't you go back where you came from?

When all is said, however, Sophie needs a job and so she
accepts Andy's offer to pay her a salary equal to what she has
been earning at the YWCA just to make lunches and goo goo
eyes at his partner to keep him working. She has no choice but
to accept, so by scene 2 Norman is typing busily in an attempt to
finish the current issue of the magazine and managing to
"smell" Sophie at the same time by ringing a little bell to
summon her from the kitchen to look up words in the dictionary.
He gets carried away, however, and starts to follow her around,
subsequently helping her to get the vacuum out of the closet,
but trying to nibble her earlobe at the same time. This behavior
sets Sophie off again, so Andy suggests that Norman go out and
buy a bottle of wine for lunch to "smooth matters over." Now,
in completely unbelievable fashion Sophie takes this
opportunity to tell Andy that she is as attracted to him as
Norman is to her—and for the *same reason*—he smells so good!
Furthermore, she says that she has explained all this to her
Marine fiancé by mail, and he has threatened to kill Andy. As
Norman returns, Andy and Sophie are in a compromising
position, kissing with complete abandon and great relish, and
Norman closes the act with: "The least you could have done was
chipped in for the wine!"

Act III finds Norman packing—*Fallout* incomplete or
not—and Andy trying in every way he can to forestall his
partner's action, finally admitting to Norman that Sophie had
kissed him because she could not resist his "smell." There is a
lot of "shtick" in this scene too, with a mock physical battle
between the two men which ends with each man landing a
karate chop on the other man's arm, midway between wrist and
elbow. In a last ditch attempt to save the magazine, Andy
handcuffs Norman to the steampipe, threatening to release him
only after he finishes the last page of the last article. This, of

course, Norman refuses to do; he will go and work for AP, while Andy will probably go back to Philadelphia and work for his father. *Fallout* is gone; Sophie has "divided and conquered." At this moment the Southern belle enters, suitcase in hand, and says that she understands Norman's feeling for her (which has now completely evaporated) since she now feels the same way about Andy. She will not marry her Marine, but will instead return to Hunnicut and practice swimming in preparation for the next Olympic competition. Andy offers her a job, at half salary, which she refuses with a speech about his lack of the ability to "feel anything" for her, and exits quickly.

Norman leaves also, but he returns at once and the two men decide to get back to work and finish the magazine. Unable to avoid the subject of Sophie, they begin to discuss her and her smell which still permeates the room, and in a completely illogical reversal of character Andy decides to go with the hippos and starts to call for Sophie, who is conveniently just outside the door. Her reason for returning (not going, really) is entirely out of character with her John Birch mentality, as she explains:

> Ah didn't get on the bus because Ah'm not goin' anywhere. Ah heard everything you said and if you were gonna give up this subversive magazine Ah was personlly gonna come in here and tear you apart mahself. Ah may not agree with what you say, but if you stop sayin' it, then no one will disagree and that is not the idea of democracy. We got free speech in this country and Ah'm here to see that it stays free and spoken.

And so the play ends with the two young men busily working on *Fallout* as Sophie "works" at sharpening pencils, making lunches, and dusting as she sings loudly *The Battle Hymn of the Republic*, joined finally by "voices from heaven," and perhaps the ACLU!

There is no doubt that there are real-life situations in which overpowering physical attraction can and does override all other considerations in a relationship. However, Norman's early statement really makes the best sense in the play. He says, "Physical attraction isn't enough. It's like chewing gum. It starts off great, but the flavor doesn't last long." And Andy's flip reply, "That's why they put five sticks in a pack" seems to indicate that both men understand what has happened and can deal with it. In actuality, however, first Norman and then Andy is powerless to behave rationally and Sophie too is drawn into the same trap. Contrary to the usual Simon play, wherein the characters have an inner consistency which lends some measure of credibility to their actions, *The Star Spangled Girl* is weakened by characters determined to undermine their validity by coming across as one-dimensional figures. The problem is that the manipulations of the playwright are patently obvious, so that at the end of the play Norman agrees to take over the role of Mrs. Machininee's escort, and Andy and Sophie will be blissfully "smelling" each other. *Fallout* meanwhile will continue to exist despite financial difficulties. As noted earlier, if the piece were to be a complete farce with no point at all, Simon might well have brought Mrs. Mackininee and Sophie's Marine onstage and perhaps coupled them as well. As it stands, the conflict between physical attraction and intellectual compatibility as bases for relationships between members of the opposite sex remains a subject still to be explored by the playwright—perhaps in a future effort.

"Visitors from Mamaroneck" — Photo by Joseph Abeles Studio
(Actors, left to right) Maureen Stapleton, George C. Scott

Plaza Suite

First presented at the Plymouth Theatre, New York City, by Saint Subber, February 14, 1968.

Director: Mike Nichols

Setting: Oliver Smith

Lighting: Jean Rosenthal

Costumes: Patricia Zipprodi

CAST

VISITORS FROM MAMARONECK

Bellhop	Bob Balaban
Karen Nash	Maureen Stapleton
Sam Nash	George C. Scott
Waiter	Jose Ocasio
Jean McCormack	Claudette Nevins

VISITOR FROM HOLLYWOOD

Waiter	Jose Ocasio
Jesse Kiplinger	George C. Scott
Muriel Tate	Maureen Stapleton

VISITORS FROM FOREST HILLS

Norma Hubley	Maureen Stapleton
Roy Hubley	George C. Scott
Borden Eisler	Bob Balaban
Mimsey Hubley	Claudette Nevins

Number of Performances: 1,097

Plaza Suite (1968)

Under the title *Plaza Suite* Neil Simon has written three short plays, unified by the use of Suite 719 in New York's Plaza Hotel as the setting common to all. In professional productions the main characters are played by the same two players, a device which is undoubtedly a source of delight for versatile performers, since the people portrayed are a different couple in each play. As the visitors come to 719, they undergo crisis-type situations, although the plays are certainly comedies if audience laughter is any yardstick. The plots are simple, and the sparkling dialogue, preposterous situations, and even farcical behavior are typical of Simon's work. However, beneath the banter and even the "shtick" we are invited to consider some matters of great seriousness, such as aging in American society, marital infidelity, the emptiness of success, non-communication, and the generation gap.

These are comedies, but in the first play we are not given the traditional happy ending, and in the other two playlets there are serious questions raised which are left unanswered. Several of the characters are somewhat exaggerated, but they remain believable because each one's behavior is "logical" for him or her, as conceived by the playwright.

There is an interesting commonality among the three principal male characters: Sam Nash, Jesse Kiplinger, and Roy Hubley. Each man has achieved the visible trappings of success as our middle-class world views that phenomenon. Each has reached the forty to fifty age bracket and somehow discovered that "winning the goal" does not necessarily bring the satisfactions associated with that feat. Sam and Jesse are determined to remain young through extra-marital sexual activity, and we feel that given the opportunity, Roy Hubley would do exactly the same thing. The wives, two of whom are also middle-aged, have "settled" with life, at least until we look at them closely. The young bride-to-be in "Forest Hills" is so afraid of becoming like her mother that she almost misses getting married at all, and the "other woman" in "Marmaroneck" is almost a stereotype of a young divorcée who has resumed her maiden name and skips dinners to maintain her slim figure. She is the efficient secretary who doubles as the boss's mistress because that is the way *she* wants it.

There are young people and children in these families although the only ones we see onstage appear in "Forest Hills." Somehow they seem disappointing to their parents, although they are also very much loved and perhaps a bit pampered.

Although there are other parallels to be drawn in the playlets, to see the underlying theme or idea in each, they must be discussed separately.

First,
"Visitors from Marmaroneck"

In this opening scene Neil Simon has created a financially comfortable middle-aged couple on the day of their twenty-third wedding anniversary. The wife, Karen Nash, is described as *"a pleasant affable woman who has let weight and age take their natural course."* Nevertheless, she is making a gallant stab at reviving the romance in her marriage by engaging 719 at the Plaza for the couple's night away from home while their house is being painted. This was the room in which the Nashes spent the first night of their honeymoon, at least as Karen recalls. She has also bought some flowers and a sexy negligee and is trying somewhat desperately to make a success of the occasion by ordering champagne and hors d'oeuvres brought to the suite. Her husband, Sam Nash, is much more concerned with his waistline, his newly capped teeth, and the denial of his age than with his wedding anniversary.

There is clever foreshadowing even before Sam enters, as Karen and the bellboy discuss tearing down old buildings and replacing them with modern monstrosities. "If it's old and beautiful, it's not there in the morning," says Karen. "Old is no good any more."

At the beginning there is some "schtick" when Karen can't get her galosh off without leaving her shoe in it, and so limps around comically, which is a bit reminiscent of the mother trying to find a pencil in *Come Blow Your Horn*. And there is a "running gag" about anchovies in the hors d'oeuvres, plus some jokes about this being the right room in the first place, but the playwright soon gets to the point. Sam's secretary, Jean McCormack, brings some papers to the hotel for Sam's signature, and she and Sam decide that they must return to the office for the evening to straighten out some details of an important business deal which is coming up the next morning. Jean is not a siren, but she is a slender twenty-eight-year old, and after she leaves, Karen jokingly asks Sam if he's having an affair with Miss McCormack. She even tells him that if what she suspects is true, it is all right. Sam denies her accusation, but we see more deeply into their life together as they agree that they "have not been happy lately." Sam tries to verbalize the cause:

> I don't know if you can understand this. But when I came home from the war I had my whole life in front of me. And all I dreamed about, all I wanted, was to get married, and to have children, and to make a success of my life. Well, I was very lucky. I got it all. Marriage, the children, more money than I ever dreamed of making. . .

And then he concludes, "I just want to do it all over again. I would like to start the whole damn thing right from the beginning."

Karen suggests that he may want "out" of their marriage, and Sam gets half-way out of the door, saying that they will discuss the problem later, when Karen quite unexpectedly explodes: "No, God dammit, we'll talk about it now. I'm not going to sit around a hotel room half the night waiting to hear how my life is going to come out."

Sam then admits his affair with Jean and is somewhat upset by Karen's sarcasm regarding his having chosen his secretary as mistress. She thinks "It's so damned unoriginal." Sam's reply, "What did you want her to be, a fighter pilot with the Israeli Air Force?" is very funny. However, the point has been made. These two people don't know each other at all. They both admit that resentments have been building up for twenty-three years. She tells him that he is vain, self-pitying, and deceiving; he tells her that she never fights back, always accepts everything in life that's thrown at her. This remark refers not only to his "affair," but also to her acceptance of middle-age and all which that connotes. Finally, Karen pleads with Sam to stay. She agrees to lie, to tell each other that everything is all right, that she is "twenty-seven God-damned years old." But he leaves without telling her when (or if) he will return. Consistent with her character, Karen says, "When? Never mind. I love surprises." The waiter enters with champagne and two glasses, and asks, "Is he coming back?" and the play closes on Karen's line, "Funny you should ask that."

There are some really great laugh lines in this piece, lines which stem from situation and character, but obviously it is a comedy in mode of writing only, since it raises some very fundamental issues and offers no pat solutions to problems shared with Karen and Sam by many middle-class, middle-aged people.

The second playlet is called
"Visitor from Hollywood"

In this playlet Neil Simon makes us laugh at the successful seduction of a young married woman by her former high school boyfriend, now a Hollywood producer of note. Muriel Tate is somewhat reluctant, or so we are led to believe at first, to visit Suite 719 and renew her relationship with the famous Jesse Kiplinger. She says she can't stay for more than a few minutes; she can't have a drink; she won't even remove her gloves. But she is very well aware of Jesse's intentions, albeit not consciously, and when he finally pretends to say goodby and allow her to leave so that she can drive back to Tenafly, New Jersey, to get dinner for her husband, it is Muriel who passionately kisses Jesse and rekindles his ardor.

"Visitor from Hollywood" — Photo by Martha Swope
(Actors, left to right) Maureen Stapleton, George C. Scott

As the scene unfolds, we find that Muriel is the typical "movie fan," who has carefully followed every gossipy detail of Jesse's life during the seventeen years since their last date. Simon pushes this right to the end of the piece when she is on the bed, having her dress unzipped, but still questioning Jesse about Hollywood personalities he has known. However, we learn quite a lot about Muriel which is a little sad. For one thing, she and her husband Larry do not have much of a marriage; he has taken over her father's business (an implied reason for the marriage to have taken place), and sometimes he doesn't come home at night. Furthermore, the lady tipples. When Jesse expresses concern about the effect of the one drink he has served her, we find that she has had two drinks before coming upstairs, and she says, "If I had to worry about getting home every time I had three vodka stingers, I'd give up driving."

Muriel has three children and a "wonderful reputation" in Tenafly, but somehow she comes across clearly as a case of arrested development, a perpetual adolescent who lives vicariously, dreaming of what it would have been like had she been able to live a more glamorous life. Her speech patterns are revealing; she undoubtedly watches soap operas slavishly and reads all movie magazines and gossip columns. For example, she goes from "Mr. Famous Producer" to "Mr. Do-Whatever-You-Want-to-Kiplinger" to "Mr. Famous Hollywood Kisser," and the playwright makes her confusion over Jesse's nickname, Pootch (because Pucci in Florence makes his shirts) and Gootch (because Gucci in Rome makes his shoes) very funny. Nevertheless, Muriel represents the kind of woman only too often found in Suburbia—not essentially a bad sort, but rather parasitic and only dimly aware that having three vodka stingers (or four or five) will not change her life permanently.

Jesse, it is obvious to the audience from the first, is out for what might be termed "a quick hit," but that isn't the most important quality of this character. He is evidently a man bored with his success. He has been married and divorced three times in fourteen years, and claims that he is still looking for a "real, honest-to-goodness, unphony woman," but Simon implies that he wouldn't recognize one if he fell over her. Muriel is impressed with his perfect record of box office hits; he says his

latest picture is "a piece of crap." The total impression we get
of Jesse is that he is a shallow person, desperately trying to
prove that he exists by an endless succession of mindless sexual
conquests.

Again, some of the dialogue is hilarious, while remaining
totally in keeping with these characters. At one point Jesse is
talking about two of his ex-wives. Muriel, of course, is
interested in hearing about the "three bitches," as Jesse labels
them, and he obliges:

> What happened? I gave them love, I gave them a home, I gave
> them a beautiful way of life—and the three bitches took me for
> every cent I got. But I don't even care about the money, screw
> it—excuse me, Muriel. What hurts is that they took the guts
> out of me. They were phony, unfaithful, all of them. Did you
> know that I caught my first wife, Dolores, in bed with a jockey?
> A jockey! Do you know what it does to a man's self-respect to
> find his wife in the sack with a four-foot-eight shrimp, weighs a
> hundred and twelve pounds? But, as I said before, screw it. Tell
> me if I'm shocking you, Muriel.

Muriel says, "I'll let you know," so Jesse continues:

> My second wife, Carlotta. She was keeping her Spanish guitar
> teacher. *Keeping* him! I never caught her but she didn't fool
> me. No one takes twenty-seven thousand dollars worth of guitar
> lessons in one year. . . .

As we would expect, Muriel isn't really interested in
whatever genuine hurt Jesse might have suffered. She asks him
only if Carlotta is the one he met at Kirk Douglas's house at a
big party for the Ukranian Folk Dancers and the Los Angeles
Rams, as reported in Sheilah Graham's column.

One of the means by which Neil Simon gets a comic effect at
the same time that he deals with a serious subject in this playlet
is that, consistent with their personalities, he makes certain that
these two people never really talk to each other at all. This is not
as apparent as the technique used in Ionesco's *Bald Soprano*,
but a careful reading or viewing of "Visitor from Hollywood"
makes it very clear that non-communication is both a cause for
laughter and an unhappy fact about much that passes for

"Visitors from Forest Hills" — Photo by Martha Swope
(Actors, left to right) Maureen Stapleton, George C. Scott

conversation between Muriel and Jesse. For instance, he tries at one point to explain to her (and by implication to all of us) that she has a very distorted image of famous Hollywood people. He gets as close to the truth as: "They're not what you think they are. *I'm* not what you think I am," but Muriel never really hears him, any more than he hears her cries for help which signify frustration with her life. These two people had known each other seventeen years earlier in Tenafly—true. But that is only an excuse for their trying to "change the world for an hour" through a sexual encounter. Jesse, we are certain, has done this many times before and will do it many times again as a means of assuring himself that he exists. Muriel will do it again too, if given the opportunity to cloak the episode with an aura of romance. These characters have individuality, but they are universal too because they represent the emptiness of many human relationships. Simon's comic presentation in a sense makes the theme even clearer than it might be if treated seriously, since there is potential for genuine intimacy between these two people who so adroitly practice self-deception and do nothing but repeat their meaningless patterns of behavior because that is all they are capable of doing. How many people suffer from this same lack of insight?

In the third playlet the characters are quite different, but just as oblivious to their real problem. It is called "Visitors from Forest Hills"

In this playlet, the suite is being used as a kind of "dressing room" for a wedding which is to take place in one of the reception rooms of the hotel. The bride-to-be, Mimsey Hubley, has locked herself in the bathroom and refuses to communicate with her parents, Norma and Roy, again the middle-aged, middle-class people so often found in Neil Simon's plays. As we would expect, this is the crisis situation. Norma and Roy are completely frustrated by their daughter's behavior: Norma because of the social implications of a cancelled wedding (She says it's the first for anyone in her family at the Plaza), and Roy because of the mounting cost of a wedding which is being delayed and delayed and delayed while guests downstairs drink his liquor, eat two hundred dollars worth of cocktail frankfurters, and listen to "four musicians playing for seventy dollars an hour."

There is more slapstick in this play than in the other two, with the concomitant necessity for a greater exaggeration of characters. As examples: Norma has several fake heart attacks; Roy ignores them. Norma tears her stockings trying to look through the keyhole of the bathroom door and then wants money from Roy to go and buy another pair before the wedding. She says, "Bergdorfs have nice stockings." Roy tries unsuccessfully to break down the bathroom door and hurts his arm; after telling her husband to move his fingers, Norma summarily dismisses the possibility that his arm is broken. Roy crawls out of the window of the sitting room to get into the bathroom that way, and Norma holds on to his rented tailcoat, which then rips completely up the back seam. Roy finds the bathroom window locked and re-enters the hotel through another guest's bedroom, but not until it has rained on him. The rain stops as suddenly as it had started, just as he returns to 719. In an attempt to prevent Roy from starting a fire to "smoke Mimsey out," Norma pounds on the door and smashes her diamond ring. When they finally do get through to their daughter, it is only to persuade her to knock once for no and twice for yes. Norma then assumes that the girl would rather talk to her than to Roy, and is crushed when Mimsey pushes a note written on toilet paper under the door. It reads, "I would rather talk to Daddy."

After she and her father have had their little conversation, Roy telephones downstairs and requests the future bridegroom, Borden Eisler, to come up at once. Roy then tells the young man that Mimsey is locked in the bathroom because she is worried about their future—about the whole institution of marriage. The completely unruffled Borden solves the problem by rapping sharply on the bathroom door, saying, "Mimsey? This is Borden. . . . Cool it!" Almost at once a radiant bride emerges and the scene closes as they leave the suite to go on with the wedding.

Since the Hubleys are less realistic than the characters in the other two playlets, some of their behavior is simply not believable if examined closely. It is quite improbable that a twenty-one year old college graduate would lock herself in the bathroom on her wedding day. And it is equally probable that if she did, either her mother or her father would have thought of a passkey, rather than having Roy crawl outside the building in an attempt to reach Mimsey. As a matter of fact, most of what happens in this segment is pure farce, a visual sort of comedy. However, even so, Neil Simon clearly makes some serious points. For one thing, neither of her parents can communicate with Mimsey. The generation gap? Secondly, Mimsey has a fear of the whole institution of marriage because she is afraid of "what they are going to become." Norma's first reaction to this remark is thoroughly conventional:

> What are they going to become? They love each other, they'll get married, they'll have children, they'll grow older, they'll become like us. . .

Then, as it states in the stage directions: *Comes the Dawn.* In reply to Roy's comment, "Makes you stop and think, doesn't it?" Norma says:

> I don't think we're so bad, do you? All right, so we yell and scream a little. So we fight and curse and aggravate each other. So you blame me for being a lousy mother and I accuse you of being a rotten husband. It doesn't mean we're not happy . . . does it? Well, does it?

Furthermore, we have hints of the Hubleys' relationship throughout the scene, despite the horseplay, and we also learn that Norma doesn't speak to *her* mother, and that Roy had turned his back to Norma when he cried in the night, thinking about losing his little girl, Mimsey. Simon always cloaks these remarks in humor, follows them with a laugh line, but they are significant. And the characters, close to caricatures as they become, do have an inner consistency which makes them recognizable to the audience and gives them dimension.

Roy is described by the playwright as *"a volatile, explosive man equipped to handle the rigors of the competitive business world, but a frightened nervous man when it comes to the business of marrying off his only daughter.* " In the sense that even a highly volatile man would be unlikely to behave as irrationally as Simon has Roy behave—yes, the character is exaggerated. However, his actions are a matter of degree, not of kind. This technique is no different from Molière's treatment of such characters as those mentioned in the first chapter of this book. We can sense in Roy Hubley all the middle-aged men who go from discomfort to panic when faced with a situation which calls for a show of emotion not socially sanctioned, men who can show anger easily but who display tenderness with difficulty.

Norma's incompetence is also overdone for the sake of humor. However, she is representative of all the middle-aged women who look forward to their daughter's wedding as the high point in their lives. We may ask what happens to the Normas of the world when this day has come and gone. Do they then concentrate on being mothers-in-law?

The parents accuse each other (humorously, of course) of having failed Mimsey, and Neil Simon suggests that this may indeed be true, but he gives no indication of how this situation could be ameliorated. Mimsey has been given a college education; she is being given an $8000 wedding. What she represents, perhaps, like the two disappointing Nash children mentioned briefly in "Visitors from Marmaroneck," is the generation of young people growing up after World War II who simply refuse to accept their parents' values, while at the same time accepting as their just due all the material advantages which their parents shower on them. Furthermore, the "communication" between Mimsey and Borden may be funny, but it is quite limited, which could augur a future problem in their lives. As to the fear of the institution of marriage itself, this is a reality for many people who are seeking less traditional ways of relating to each other, even in the middle-class society of which Simon writes.

In *Plaza Suite* the characters are memorable because, with the possible exception of Jean McCormack, they are unique individuals, still retaining a universality by representing an entire group of people. If Sam Nash, Jesse Kiplinger, and Roy Hubley share some problems, as noted earlier, this does not mean that the playwright merely presents cardboard images of three prosperous men who find middle-age disappointing. It is evident that the Nashes are more sophisticated than the Hubleys. It is clear that succeeding as a Hollywood producer is quite different from succeeding as a New York business man. Therefore, it is logical that Sam Nash can verbalize more easily than Roy Hubley, and that Jesse Kiplinger is the most articulate of the three men, as well as the phoniest.

If we examine the three wives, we see that only Norma Hubley has gone the whole way in playing the role of conventional wife-mother. She and Roy are not really happy, but "that's the way it goes." Karen Nash would gladly accept the same role, but she has enough insight to understand that her life is not working well and to be concerned about it. She is willing to do anything to keep Sam. Muriel Tate is still in her thirties, but she has already discovered that doing what society in Tenafly expects a wife-and-mother-of-three to do is not satisfying. So she lives in an unrealistic world, colored by vodka stingers. At any rate, all of these characters have enough verisimilitude, in spite of some exaggeration for the sake of comedy, to function as conduits through which the playwright's serious themes flow.

Last of the Red Hot Lovers

First presented at the Eugene O'Neill Theatre, New York City, by Saint Subber, December 28, 1969.

Director: Robert Moore

Setting: Oliver Smith

Lighting: Peggy Clark

Costumes: Donald Brooks

CAST

Barney Cashman . . . . James Coco
Elaine Navazio . . . . Linda Lavin
Bobbi Michele . . . . Marcia Rodd
Jeanette Fisher . . . . Doris Roberts

Number of Performances: 706

Last Of The Red Hot Lovers — Photo by Joseph Abeles Studio
(Actors, left to right) Linda Lavin, James Coco

Last of the Red Hot Lovers (1969)

In this play the action is again divided into three segments, but instead of separate sets of characters, Simon has created one pivotal man, Barney Cashman, and three women, each one appearing in one act of the play. Elaine Navazio, Bobbi Michele, and Jeanette Fisher are humorously contrasted and each has her effect on the protagonist. The themes? Once more we are asked to consider the frustrations of approaching middle-age, non-communication, the generation gap, and even whether or not we are truly alive or just pretending that we are.

To ensure that this play will be a comedy, the playwright has selected a setting which is in itself fraught with hazards, since Barney Cashman has decided to use his mother's place for romantic adventure. Now Barney's mother lives in a small modern apartment—with a convertible sofa, paper thin walls, and a nosey neighbor. Therefore, when this forty-seven year old owner of a fish restaurant, who has never been unfaithful to his wife in their twenty-three years of marriage, decides to take advantage of his mother's absence two afternoons a week (she does charity work at Mt. Sinai Hospital) he brings his own liquor and even glasses, for fear that Mrs. Cashman, Sr. will notice that he's been there and wonder why. Typically for his kind of personality, Barney worries about everything from the way the pillows on the couch are plumped to the sound of voices which might arouse suspicion with the neighbor. And since his mother always returns precisely at five o'clock, the time factor is also used for comic effect. As we would expect, there are "running gags" in each act, but these in no way detract from Neil Simon's rather serious conclusion: an affirmation of our shared humanity, which is something different from the traditional "happy ending" for a comedy.

Soon after Barney has opened the play by calling his restaurant and telling his cashier that he is shopping at Bloomingdale's, we meet Elaine Navazio, described by the playwright as *"a somewhat attractive woman in her late thirties, having an air of desperation about her."* She is married, drinks heavily, smokes, coughs, and frequently and frankly indulges in casual sexual encounters because, as she tells Barney, the act "warms me—stimulates me—and makes me feel like a woman."

Barney Cashman is basically a very decent person, concerned with people from "trivia to tragedy," as he would affirm in the alliterative style of his restaurant's menus. (Succulent Savory Swordfish Steak and Flaming Florentine Flounder are two of his efforts). He enjoys opening clams and oysters every morning, but he worries constantly about the fishy odor which returns to his fingers each afternoon "like the tide coming in." He has a wife, three children, and a reasonably successful business; he also has a conservative way of dressing, although he assures Elaine that he does have several sports jackets in his closet. Above all, he has a completely uneventful life. He is so *nice* that nothing noteworthy has ever happened to him, and at forty-seven he suddenly wonders if anything ever will. Actually, he's been thinking for some time about having one memorable "affair," and it is this dream which has triggered his invitation to Elaine. She, however, is more than a little impatient with Barney's adolescent idea of a romantic interlude, preceded by "human communication." He wants romance; she wants to "get laid." As she says, "You need Joan Fontaine and [because of her cough] I need a box of lozenges."

There is a great deal of comic repartee between these two people, based on the setting, the situation, and their incompatibility. For example, there is the "running gag" about Elaine's desire for cigarettes. Barney, of course, is a non-smoker. And there is some slapstick too, although it is not a major component. Mainly, there is the serious dialogue between Barney and Elaine at the end. It's not a conversation, really, but a verbal battle. Barney tries to explain what he himself does not fully understand: his desire to "live" before he is officially declared dead. Elaine's initial impulse is to leave with a

wisecrack, after he's told her that she's "flippant, wise, cold
. . . callous and unemotional," but when he adds, "pitiful," she
comes back into the apartment and tells him what a hypocrite
she thinks he is. Then she says:

> I don't know your problems and I don't care. . . . No one really
> cares about anything or anyone in this world except himself,
> and there's only one way to get through with your sanity. If you
> can't taste it, touch it, or smell it, forget it!

And adds:

> . . . no one gives a good crap about you dying because a lot of
> people have discovered it ahead of you. We're all dying, Mr.
> Cashman. As a matter of fact, I myself passed away about six
> months ago.

As the act closes, Barney vows aloud never to repeat this
experience, but the next act, which takes place eight months
later, finds Barney again in his mother's apartment, greeting
the second female character, Bobbi Michele.

In this encounter much of the comedy stems from Bobbi's
complete kookiness. We learn that "some kind man" had
loaned her money to pay an accompanist for an audition, and
then we find that she has come to this apartment without even
being certain that Barney is her benefactor. She doesn't listen
to a thing Barney says, but spouts constantly, senselessly,
about the cab driver who had wanted to "make it with her"
under the Manhattan Bridge during his lunch hour; the Chinese
man on the plane from California who kept "feeling her up" all
during the movie, and didn't even have his earphones plugged
in; the unknown caller who had left an obscene message on her
telephone answering machine when she wasn't at home, and
anecdotes of this kind. The unbelievable tales build up, and
Barney, living vicariously, is fascinated by them. And no
wonder, since Bobbi's stories include a Hollywood weirdo with
sharpened teeth, a mysterious beating by some "Mexican in a
motel," a political bigwig who had had her dog kidnapped, and
the Nazi lesbian vocal teacher with black shirts, boots, and a

Last Of The Red Hot Lovers — Photo by Joseph Abeles Studio
(Actors, left to right) James Coco, Marcia Rodd

leather bedspread with whom she now lives. The girl insists that she is here to repay the twenty dollars which Barney had loaned her, but when he reluctantly agrees to accept the money, she tells him that she doesn't have it, but she's "good for it" because if she doesn't get a show in New York, she may do a series of one-night concerts in New Zealand. Finally, she asks Barney if he minds her smoking, and this time, after his experience with Elaine, he is prepared—or thinks he is—by having a selection of brands. Bobbi, however, doesn't mean tobacco; she means marijuana. And she wants Barney to "turn on" with her.

In keeping with his character, Barney pretends he has smoked "pot" and is just trying to cut down. Bobbi reassures him by saying that these sticks are a prescription from a Beverly Hills doctor, to be taken in place of tranquilizers. After she has had one joint, her stories get even wilder, and we can understand (as Barney must) that Bobbi Michele is a bonafide mental case. At any rate, she decides to have one more smoke before leaving and almost bludgeons Barney into joining her. The resulting scene is hilarious as Bobbi tells him to swallow the smoke, which he does. The problem comes when he tries to exhale it and nothing comes out. The girl assures him that in a few minutes his mouth will feel numb and his toes will start to tingle. He replies, "Good, good. I can't wait." Barney does indeed get "high" and follows Bobbi's advice to just go with the feeling and "let it all hang out." However, the girl's final speech is somewhat parallel to Elaine Navazio's as she says:

> You've got to make it alone in this world. All I need is one good show. The talent's there; it's just a question of time. . . . People don't want to see you make good. They're all jealous. . . They're all rotten . . . they're all vicious.

Meanwhile, Barney, convinced that he is dying, replies with a non sequitur:

> So many things I wanted to do . . . but I'll never do 'em. So many places I wanted to see. . . . I'll never see 'em. Trapped! We're all trapped. . . . HELP! HELP!

which is a statement with an internal truth all its own. Barney and so many other people find themselves "trapped," sane, perhaps, in an insane world.

Significant to the development of the main character is the short time lapse between Acts II and III—only one month this time, and for this third assignation Barney is gaily dressed in one of the sports jackets he had mentioned to Elaine in Act I and wears what Simon indicates is *"a joyful tie."* This time he has brought champagne too. Enter Jeanette Fisher, a lady who projects from the moment Barney opens the door only one characteristic: utter depression.

We soon learn that she and her husband, Mel, have been close friends of the Cashmans for years, and Barney also learns almost immediately that Jeanette does *not* feel physically attracted to him. Taking this in stride because of the "nice" man that he is, Barney is next confronted by the fact that for the past eight months Mel has slept with Jeanette, but she has not slept with him! She doesn't care for sex, she says, because nothing is very important to her anymore. She is in analysis for melancholia, and she explains to Barney that she has actually figured out the percentage of her life which might be called "the happiness factor." It is 8.2%. Jeanette takes pills for her depression, she tells him, and when she and Dr. Margolies think she's ready, she's going to get into her car and drive off the Verrazano Bridge! Much of this conversation is hilarious and there is more than a suggestion of Molière in the portion of the dialogue which deals with Jeanette's insistence that Barney name three decent, gentle, loving people. He names Jesus, JFK, and his wife, Thelma, but within a few moments, Jeanette has reversed the situation and raised Barney's suspicions about Thelma's "decency."

Throughout the act there is a constant joke about Jeanette's purse; she won't put it down, but clings to it like a security blanket. And Simon gets some mileage out of Barney's increasingly drastic oaths to convince Jeanette about his silence re their rendezvous. He assures her that he will never "kiss and tell," or even tell since there has been no kissing, and finally reaches a high point with, "May I have a coronary occlusion in my doctor's office!"

Last Of The Red Hot Lovers — Photo by Joseph Abeles Studio
(Actors, left to right) James Coco, Doris Roberts

Jeanette must now take a pill without water because she is too depressed to wait for a drink, but her explanation calls for more than laughter. She says:

Isn't that how we cope with our problems today, Barney? With pills, drugs. . . . Do you know how many people in this country take pills because they cannot cope with emotional problems?

And we learn a lot about excuses for culpable behavior in this modern society too, as Jeanette tells Barney how her husband, Mel, had forbidden her to continue her friendship with Mrs. Charlotte Korman, and then confessed to having an affair with that lady. She speaks of his rationale, delivered at two o'clock one morning:

. . . He explained it to me. We're living in a guiltless society. You can do anything you want as long as you're honest about it. Aren't we lucky to be living in such a civilized age? In the old days I would have gone to my grave ignorant of the wonderful and beautiful knowledge that my husband was spending his afternoons humping Charlotte Korman.

As Jeanette is about to leave, without having had their "affair," of course, Barney makes a rapid transition from mouse to lion, as he insists that Jeanette admit that he is not an *indecent* person. As he puts it, "Foolish, stupid, maybe, but I'm not *indecent!*" She replies that she'll lie and admit they are a terrific bunch of people, which logically triggers his response:

All right! All right, we're all no good. We're all indecent, un-feeling, unloving, rotten human beings. Sick, monstrous, disgusting people, all of us.

And he recaps his experiences with Elaine and Bobbi, explaining in his way that "nothing happened" in either encounter because he had been looking for "something beauti-ful, something decent." Then he continues:

. . . I'm through, dammit. I'm through looking for something beautiful and decent because *it doesn't exist.* You're right, Jeanette, we're no damned good, all of us. There are no decent, gentle, loving people left in the world. We're depraved, lustful, disgusting monsters, all of us. But if we're guilty, Jeanette, then let's see a little depravity. If we're indecent, then let's see a couple of terrific indecencies.

As he speaks, Barney stalks Jeanette around the room, overturning chairs, and finally convincing her that he is dead serious. He paraphrases Elaine with "I'm not interested in your troubles. I want your flesh, not your heartbreaking stories," and Jeanette is beginning to believe he means it. She keeps saying that he is really not like this, so he asks her to tell him what he is really like. All of this conversation is punctuated with Barney giving an excellent imitation of a potential rapist.

At last the tearful woman admits that Barney is quiet, intelligent and *decent.* He is also gentle and loving. And Neil Simon (through Barney) pushes home the point. If there is one such person, logically there must be more. Jeanette is confused by the rapidly changing world, but as she admits—deep down she does believe as he does that not all people are sick and rotten; some are decent, gentle and loving.

After Jeanette's exit with a funny line about waking Mel at two o'clock in the morning to "confess that she has had an affair . . . Let him be depressed for a while," Barney straightens up the overturned furniture and gets an idea. He telephones his wife, Thelma, and asks her to meet him if she's not too busy. The playwright, however, avoids the obvious cliché of having Thelma agree without argument, so that "all is well." Instead, Barney's final line is, "Thelma, don't be so stubborn. Can't you meet me in my mother's apartment?" And he's still on the phone as the curtain comes down.

In *Last of the Red Hot Lovers* we have once again rather average, middle-class people, with the exception of Bobbi, who might have started life that way, perhaps as one of the "ungrateful" children of the 1960's. They are all having difficulty coping with a world in flux (not a topical matter, as even a cursory glance at history will show), and each one is dealing with that world in a way logical for that individual. Through these characters Neil Simon has dealt with non-communication, marriages which leave a great deal to be desired, and to some extent, expectation and wish-fulfillment as opposed to reality. Even Elaine wishes Barney good luck in his quest for the Impossible Dream.

The Gingerbread Lady

First presented at the Plymouth Theatre, New York City, by Saint Subber, December 13, 1970.

Director: Robert Moore

Setting: David Hays

Lighting: Martin Aronstein

Costumes: Frank Thompson

CAST

Jimmy Perry	Michael Lombard
Manuel	Alex Colon
Toby Landau	Betsy von Furstenberg
Evy Meara	Maureen Stapleton
Polly Meara	Ayn Ruymen
Lou Tanner	Charles Siebert

Number of Performances: 193

The Gingerbread Lady — Photo by Joseph Abeles Studio
(Actors, left to right) Betsy von Furstenberg, Ayn Ruymen,
Maureen Stapleton, Michael Lombard

The Gingerbread Lady (1970)

Essentially a drama rather than a comedy, this play is humorous only to the extent that there is some funny dialogue stemming very naturally from characters who live in a world where wisecracks serve to mask almost constant cries for help. It was not originally written to close as it does, and it works very effectively when the tacked-on "happy ending" is omitted. It is significant that many drama critics "panned" or at least did not enthusiastically praise the play even after the ending had been altered, on the assumption that this playwright could and should create only comedy, which makes it quite clear that there has been little critical recognition of Simon's underlying seriousness.

With no need to exaggerate for comic effect, the characters in this play seem particularly well-drawn. The protagonist, Evy Meara, is not patterned after a famous singer (although there were critical hints that she was meant to portray the late Judy Garland), for Evy never had made the big-time. What she does represent is the universal character who cannot walk through life without the crutch of alcohol, an ephemeral prop at best. Evy is surrounded by others: Jimmy Perry, Lou Tanner, and Toby Landau, all "losers" too, which adds reality, since it is quite common for people to associate with others not unlike themselves.

Jimmy Perry is a homosexual, an unsuccessful actor in his early forties, who suspects, but cannot admit, that his chance for becoming a star has passed, if it ever existed at all. Lou Tanner is a crude stud, who hides his genuine talent for using other people behind his pretended talent for musical composition. He can play the guitar passably well, but he cannot compete in the creative arena. Toby Landau is the "eternal beauty queen," whose life has always revolved around herself with the main emphasis on her outward appearance. She seems somewhat overdrawn until Simon reveals her motivation for narcissism in the last act.

The only "winner" is Polly, Evy's teenage daughter, who has been living with her father and stepmother since her parents' divorce seven years earlier. She is almost an idealized character, probably representative of what most middle-aged parents want to believe their teenagers are really like beneath their apparent disinterest in everything except sex and rock music. Polly has a frankness typical of the "bra-less generation," and she has a lot of love to give. If she seems somewhat more perceptive than a seventeen-year old might be expected to be, perhaps this can be legitimately attributed to the life she's led. After all, Evy has been an alcoholic neurotic for a number of years (twenty, according to Lou Tanner), so it is logical to assume that Polly has had to mature early simply to survive. She knows the score, as we can see when she reminds her mother early in the play of a treasured gift Evy had given her eight years before:

> Don't you remember the Gingerbread House with the little gingerbread lady in the window? I have always kept it to remind me of you. Of course, today I have the biggest box of crumbs in the neighborhood. Come on, be a sport. Buy me another one this Christmas.

Tragically, the gingerbread lady crumbles again, and it is clear that Evy will repeat this pattern endlessly despite any good intentions to the contrary. Therefore, it is consistent with Polly's character that she is finally forced to recognize the futility of trying to "save" her mother, a decision which the playwright undoubtedly had in mind when creating his original third-act curtain.

The action or plot, like that of most Neil Simon's plays, is relatively straightforward. We are introduced to all the characters in Act I, as Jimmy Perry waits for Toby Landau to bring Evy home from a ten-week stay in a sanitarium where she had been taken after being found floating face down in her bathtub. The apartment, a third floor brownstone in the West Eighties, has *"fallen into disrepair,"* and the furniture, complete with a small, battered piano, sets the stage for the depressing world of the has-been nightclub singer, Evy Meara. Jimmy is trying valiantly to make the place cheerful with a bowl of fresh flowers as he is interrupted by the arrival of a delivery boy with groceries. The Puerto Rican youngster refuses Jimmy's explanation that Mrs. Meara has a "charge account" and impudently demands $14.28 in cash, which Jimmy finally digs up, but not before the boy has caught sight of his unemployment book, which places Jimmy for the audience.

Finally, Toby arrives with the "new" Evy Meara, forty-two pounds and twenty-seven hundred dollars lighter than when she had left, but still quite obviously a very high-strung woman who covers her neurosis with one quip after another—albeit never quite successfully. For instance, when Toby offers to loan her money until she "gets started again," Evy answers, "Work? Singing in clubs? The last job I had was two years ago in Pittsburgh. I broke the house record. Fell off the stool seventeen times in one show." Then, she continues to denigrate herself with, "I shared a dressing room with a female impersonator who had the hots for me. I think we made it but I forget which way."

Almost at once Toby has to leave for a dinner with her husband, and when Jimmy follows soon after to audition for a part in an off-Broadway show, we get the feeling that Evy will have a really hard time being alone even for a little while. Just as she nears the point of no control, her daughter, Polly, arrives with a suitcase and the announcement that she has her father's permission to live with her mother. At this point Evy's fear of failing the girl comes through clearly, covered as always by smart-aleck talk. She says she won't be good at "mothering." As she tells it:

> I was feeling very motherly one time. I bought a couple of turtles, two for eighty-five cents, Irving and Sam. I fed them once. In the morning they were floating on their backs. I don't think I could go through that again. . . . What kind of influence would I be on you? I talk filthy. I have always talked filthy. I'm a congenital filthy talker.

She then goes on to tell Polly about her relationship with Lou Tanner, which is no surprise to the girl, who refuses to be shocked. Her final response, "I don't want to judge you, Evy. I just want to live with you," however, is not enough for her mother. So Evy goes on:

> You're seventeen years old; it's time you judged me. I just don't want you to get the idea that a hundred and eighty-three pounds of pure alcohol is something called Happy Fat. . . . Many a night I would have thrown myself out that window if I could have squeezed through. I'm not what you'd call an emotionally stable person. You know how many times I was *really* in love since your father and I broke up? I met the only man who ever meant anything to me about seven, maybe eight times. Mr. Right I meet at least twice a week. I sure know true love when I see it. It's wherever I happen to look.

This speech, of course, gives the audience an added view of Evy; she apparently uses sex as she does alcohol in her effort to survive. At this juncture also we learn that the guitar player, Lou Tanner, had abruptly deserted Evy in favor of an "eighteen-year-old firm-bodied little Indian hippie," a rejection which had prompted her attempted suicide. But all promises to be different as mother and daughter begin to plan a new life together.

Almost immediately, Lou strolls in and quite brashly suggests that Evy forgive and forget so that they can resume their former relationship. Determined to stay on the wagon and out of trouble, she replies in typical Simonesque speech:

> Lou, I'm forty-three years old and I'm trying to be a grown-up lady. The doctor told me I'm not allowed to drink anymore or have affairs with thirty-three year old guitar players. . . . I thank you for your visit. Now go home, find someone your own age and light up some Astro-Turf or whatever you're smoking these days.

Somewhat scoffingly, he tries to persuade her by saying:

What are you going to tell me, you're cured? You had butter-
milk for twelve weeks and now you'll live happily ever after?
There's still a whole life to get through, Evy. . . . Together,
Evy, we don't add up to one strong person, I just think together
we have a better chance.

Glancing toward the bedroom, she resolutely refuses. "What I
need now is a relative, not a relationship. And I have one in
there unpacking," she says. So Lou leaves. Polly offers to
repack her suitcase, if that is her mother's choice, but Evy
remains firm, closing the act with lines entirely suitable to a
dutiful parent: "If you're unpacked, then wash your hands, set
the table and light the stove. It's dinnertime. And none of that
Evy crap. . . I'm your mother. I want a little respect, for crise
sakes!"

Early in Act II, which takes place three weeks later, Simon
brings his major characters together again, but this time their
skins are quickly peeled back, so that their inner selves stand
revealed—battered, bloody, and somewhat sickening. They do,
however, always have Simon's empathy, even when they're
"indecent," in the sense that Barney Cashman uses that word,
so their creator never becomes judgmental or incompassionate.

We see at the very beginning of the act that Polly is
concerned about her mother having tumbled from the wagon,
since the teenager is on the telephone calling a bar to ask about
Evy's possible whereabouts. And that lady *is* quite late. But
when she comes home, she is very happy, claiming that her
"high" is the result of having met an old girl friend whose
husband will give her a job as hostess in one of his four
restaurants. Now, she tells Polly, she feels "alive, noticed, and
even wanted." However, she does let it slip that she celebrated
by having a sherry at lunch, but promises only to *pour* the
champagne she has bought for Toby's birthday party, not to
taste it. There is almost an argument about Evy's feeling that
her daughter is acting like a "seventeen-year-old cop," but the
party mood is restored as Polly reminds her mother of the
luncheon scheduled with Mr. Meara the next day at Rumpelmayer's, "just to see how things are going." With the arrival of
the guests, however, the occasion quickly becomes funereal.

Jimmy is the first one; he is obviously very shaken and quite

different from the flippant character of the first act. We find
that he has been fired by the "nineteen-year-old putz producer" just three days before the play's opening. His
explanation is searing and shows the depth of his desperation:

> You know how it feels for a grown man to plead and beg to a
> child, Evy? *A child!* I said to him, 'You're not happy. I'll do it
> any way you want. Faster, slower, louder. I'll wear a dress. I'll
> shave my head. I'll relieve myself on the stage in front of my
> own family! I'm an actor, give me a chance to act! . . . He
> turned his back on me and shoved a Tootsie Roll in his mouth.

From this speech Jimmy goes on to a complete breakdown, sobs
and all, which has a devastating effect on Evy. As she tries to
console her friend by assuring him that he's a good actor, she
takes a drink of champagne, which brings him to the realization
that he isn't the only person with a serious problem. Evy
assures him that she is only "sipping," and they both decide to
put on a cheerful act for the birthday girl who is expected
momentarily.

Toby, in a new dress and a façade of bravado, arrives
without her husband, revealing almost at once that her world
has also crashed without warning; Martin is packing to leave
her. No, it's not another woman, she announces; he has merely
decided that he's devoid of sexual desire for her and intends to
seek a divorce. Her great need for self-justification calls forth an
almost chronological recital of experiences she has had with
men—men who had found her beauty irresistible—and as she
reaches a crescendo of near-hysteria, it becomes more and more
obvious that this woman has always concentrated on and valued
what is essentially worthless—her outward appearance—and
neglected completely the development of an inner self with
which to deal with life, particularly life at age forty.
She begins:

> Did you know . . . that in 1950 I was voted the prettiest girl at
> the University of Michigan? An All-American halfback was
> willing to give up a trip to the Rose Bowl for one night of my
> favors. . . . In 1951 I switched schools and was voted the
> prettiest girl at the University of Southern California. . . . I re-

ceived on the average of fifteen sexual proposals a week, at least two from the faculty.

Then, she goes on through an offer at sixteen (apparently before the college experiences) from R.K.O. Pictures, who didn't care that she couldn't act. "They said the way I looked," she says, "it wasn't important." Some of this is obviously fictional, as is evident from her next segment:

> When I was seventeen years old, a married psychiatrist in Los Angeles drove his car into a tree because I wouldn't answer his phone calls. You can read all of this in my diaries; I still have them. When I was nineteen I had an affair with a boy who was the son of the largest book publisher in the world. . . When I was twenty, I had an affair *with* the largest book publisher in the world. . . The son threatened to kill the father, but by then I was having an affair with the youngest symphony conductor in the world.

And, as she accelerates, she ranges farther and farther from reality:

> When I was twenty-three, I *slept* with a member of the British Royal Household. I slept with him *in* the British Royal House. There is a Senator living in Washington, D.C. today, who will vote any way I want him to vote by spending just one morning in Washington, D.C. . . .

And she goes on and on, desperately trying to convince herself that she is still "young, attractive, desirable." Simon's dialogue is funny, some of it, but the serious undertone is there. Her pathetic attempt at self-deception becomes especially clear as she tells of a rather recent experience:

> Last December in Los Angeles, that boy I had an affair with, the book publisher's son, called me at the Beverly Hills Hotel, *dying* to see me. He came over and we had cocktails in the Polo Lounge. He looked like my father, my *father,* Evy. And then the waiter came over, and I swear, the waiter asked for my I.D. card. . . . I know it's dark in the Polo Lounge, but it's not *that* dark.

Finally, Toby gets to the crux of her situation as she asserts doggedly that femininity and beauty are the qualities desired above all others by all men, and then trails off with, "But if it no longer interests Martin, I assure you, somewhere soon, someplace, someone else will be very . . . very . . . very . . . interested." The plea for succor is followed first by an almost audible silence, and then by an announcement by Evy that "For purely medicinal purposes, I'm having a drink."

As this dreadful excuse for a "celebration" goes on, Evy continues to drink, disregarding warnings from Jimmy, Toby, and even Polly. And we see this woman for what she really is—an intelligent, witty person bent on self-destruction. She relies on liquor to give her a sense of worth, to make her feel "wanted," to help her cope with her existence. The portrait is very clear, all-too-accurate, and deeply tragic. As Neil Simon suggests in his stage directions, *"Once on alcohol, she enters a world of her own,"* and since it is a world which her friends cannot bear to share at this time in their lives, they leave, each sincerely regretful for having triggered Evy's return to the bottle but also quite angry with her—really for being Evy Meara, acknowledged alcoholic.

She continues to drink, almost begging her daughter to come out of the bedroom and be with her, but the girl is too hurt by her mother's behavior to respond, so Act II closes with a very drunk Evy, determined not to be alone, telephoning Lou Tanner and inviting herself to his place.

The next morning (Act III) Polly and Toby are waiting for Evy, who has not been home all night. Polly finally lets herself be persuaded to lie down and rest just before her mother comes in, beaten up and sporting a shiner given her by her ex-boyfriend. She admits that it "hurts like Hell," but adds, "It sure beats indifference." Then, as Toby attempts to chide her, the two women really level with each other. Toby, of course, fears encroaching age, to which Evy replies:

> Why don't you spend the rest of your life in the Beverly Hills Polo Lounge? You can put on a Shirley Temple dress and suck a lollipop. . . . And next year you'll have an affair with the book publisher's grandson.

And in turn Toby says:

> You're an alcoholic with no sense of morality or responsibility.
> You've never had a lasting relationship with anyone who wasn't
> as weak or helpless as yourself. So you have friends like Jimmy
> and me. We all hold each other up because none of us has the
> strength to do it alone.

Then, as she verbalizes the motivation for her constant concern
with her beauty, she also restates the playwright's basic
premise in regard to these characters: low self-esteem is their
common denominator and its effects are deadly. She says:

> I know what I am, Evy. *I don't like it and I never have.* So I
> cover the outside with Helena Rubenstein. I use little makeup
> jars, you use quart bottles. And poor Jimmy uses a little of
> both. . . . Some terrific people.

This brings her to consider the one person who still has a
chance, Polly, and so she tells Evy that she must make a
decision. "Either get a book on how to be a mature, responsible
person or get her out of here before you destroy her chance to
become one." Knowing that what Toby has said is true, Evy
accepts her friend's criticism, and with a hug, gives her some
advice in return. "Go home, wash the crap off your face, put on
a sloppy housedress and bring him a TV dinner. What the hell
could you lose?"

Toby then exits, promising to "blow up the beauty parlor"
on her way home, leaving Polly and her mother to have a scene
during which the girl admits having taken a drink or two in the
morning to make her throbbing head stop hurting. The mood
becomes almost tender as Polly shows her understanding of her
mother's addiction when she asks seriously, "Is that what it's
like, Evy? Is that what it does? Makes things more bearable?"
And Evy agrees that "If you take enough, it even stops the
throbbing. . . ." But Evy resumes her flippant attitude as soon
as Polly reminds her of their date with Mr. Meara at Rumpelmayer's. To mask her fear, she says:

EVY: What lunch date?. . . Are you serious? With me look-
            ing like Rocky Graziano? He'll send you to a convent.
POLLY: We could put something on it. Some powder or some-
            thing. Or you could wear a hat. With a little veil.
EVY: I could sit behind a big screen and talk through a
            microphone. I can't go to Rumpelmayer's looking like
            this.
POLLY: . . .How about you just did a Tareyton commercial?
EVY: How about just forgetting it?
POLLY: We can't. He's expecting you. What about a pair of
            dark sunglasses?
EVY: It's not just the eye, baby. I have a hangover and the
            shakes. When I start spilling water on his lap, he's
            gonna notice something.

Going through with this commitment is quite beyond Evy's
capacity, and Polly's insistence makes the central issue very
clear. The girl wants her mother to accept this incident as a
setback and continue the fight; Evy doesn't have the strength to
remain in the ring. Polly fears that a delay will be fatal—that
she will be "all grown up." As she puts it, "Is it such a God-
damned big deal to need somebody? If you can need a bottle of
Scotch or a Lou Tanner, why can't you need me?" But Evy
knows she will only *use* the girl, as she has "used" her friends,
and mercifully sends her away—despite all Polly's objections—
permanently.

   The phone rings; Evy doesn't answer it. Jimmy comes to the
door; Evy won't let him in. She takes a bottle out of her coat
pocket, pours herself a drink, and starts her return to oblivion.
Jimmy insists on entering, actually breaking down the door,
vows vengeance on Lou Tanner when he sees Evy's battered
face, and tries ineffectually to help her "get through" this
crisis. With complete truth of characterization, Simon has Evy
send him away too, and, as the play originally ended, Evy is left
in the darkened apartment playing an old recording of hers and
lifting another glass of whiskey in a mocking gesture of toasting
herself. Tragedy? Yes, emphatically yes.

   During the road tryouts critics did not take kindly to a Neil
Simon play with this negative conclusion, and the playwright
was persuaded to write a more upbeat ending before the

Broadway opening. With the traditional conclusion for a comedy (so designated because everything turns out well for the protagonist), Polly returns; she and Evy have words; the girl smashes her mother's glass, after which Evy agrees to put makeup on her black eye and keep the appointment for lunch. However, even in this version, Evy's curtain line (spoken to Polly), "When I grow up, I want to be just like you," has significance in Neil Simon's portrait of this woman because Evy will never grow up—that's the whole problem. When she is sober, she has a delightful if somewhat Rabelaisian sense of humor, a quick mind, an honesty and largesse in her relationship with other people. But she also has an over-whelming need to destroy herself, a self-loathing at her core which is the basis for her addiction, and which dooms her to endless repetition of her immature behavior. It is not very probable that even with Polly's support she would go to lunch with her ex-husband and place herself in a vulnerable position, particularly after the night she's just gone through. It is much more in keeping with her personality, as Simon has drawn it, to have her salve her wounds in the old familiar way, by sitting in the darkened room with a bottle until she passes out.

In *The Gingerbread Lady* the playwright has created characters through whom he deals with alcoholism, parent-child relationship, friendship based on mutual weakness and need, and the waste of life itself, all subjects considered appropriate for serious drama. In certain respects this play has a somewhat Chekhovian quality in that its people are funny at one level, deeply tragic at another. They are pitiful because they are not actively rebelling against the circumstances and weaknesses which imprison them, but instead seem resigned to beating their fists against the bars until their knuckles are bloody in empty gestures which presage failure. All of them, even Toby, will quite probably continue to live hopeless, frustrating lives. Only Polly can escape if she closes the door to Evy Meara's apartment and turns resolutely and without a backward glance toward Rumpelmayer's.

Prisoner Of Second Avenue — Photo by Martha Swope
(Actors, left to right) Peter Falk (seated), Lee Grant
(standing)

Prisoner of Second Avenue

First presented at the Eugene O'Neill Theatre, New York City, by Saint Subber, November 11, 1971.

Director: Mike Nichols

Setting: Richard Sylbert

Lighting: Tharon Musser

Costumes: Anthea Sylbert

CAST

Mel Edison	Peter Falk
Edna Edison	Lee Grant
Harry Edison	Vincent Gardenia
Pearl	Florence Stanley
Jessie	Tresa Hughes
Pauline	Dena Dietrich

Number of Performances: 780

Prisoner of Second Avenue (1971)

If we take an optimistic view of the world, this could well be Neil Simon's most topical play, since we can hope that the shambles in which most urban dwellers currently find themselves will seem unbelievable to future generations simply because drastic ameliorations will have taken place. However, since the quality of life has not improved in the years since the play was first produced, but has actually deteriorated, the door of the jail in which "the prisoner" finds himself will probably remain locked for a great while to come. Meanwhile, it may be that this very funny play dealing with crowding, crime, and unemployment makes more cogent comment on the ills of twentieth century society than many plays purported to be dramas. In addition to these broad problems of social concern, Simon also considers here relationships within a family, always a universal theme.

The characters, particularly the main characters, are not so much larger than life as to lose credibility (except for the Voice of the Newscaster, a device which stresses and exaggerates current events for a purely comic effect). And all of these people are urbane Simonesque New Yorkers who can behave hilariously on one level, while projecting simultaneously the serious subtext which the playwright wishes to get across.

There are a great many jokes in *Prisoner* based on such prosaic items as the weather, the paper thin walls, the poorly functioning toilet, and the neighbors. The funny lines tumble out so quickly that they hardly give the audience a chance to stop laughing. Once again, however, even the conclusion which the playwright provides for the protagonist is merely a temporary vent for frustration—a bandaid for the cancer—nothing more. So we may conclude that Neil Simon is not offering an easy solution for the problems of his characters, nor, by extension, for us, but is perhaps hopeful that by pointing them out to us, he may cause us to look for solutions.

The action begins in the middle of a stifling summer night in the apartment of Mel and Edna Edison, Second Avenue, New York City. Mel can't sleep and is soon joined by his wife who tries to assuage his anguish in every way she can. Every trifle is "getting to him": the air conditioner which keeps the apartment too cold for comfort; the noise of the city, loud even at 2:30 a.m. on the fourteenth floor; the continually partying stewardesses who live next door; his stomach which is protesting his "health food" lunch; a barking dog; and the odor of garbage which has not been collected due to a strike. Mel's line, "This country is being buried by its own garbage." elicits the expected response—recognition—and sets the tone for the play. Simon goes on from there.

We become aware that there is more than surface irritation involved in Mel's insomnia when he tells his wife:

> Something is happening to me. . . . I'm losing control. I can't handle things any more. The telephone on my desk rings seven, eight times before I answer it. . . . I forgot how to work the water cooler today. I stood there with an empty cup in my hand and water running all over my shoes.

What a perfect example of a comic image masking a very serious idea! Edna tries to tell her husband that everyone feels tension, but his answer is frightening. He explains:

> If I could just feel tension, I'd give a thousand dollars to charity. When you're tense, you're tight, you're holding on to something. I don't know where to grab, Edna. I'm slipping and I'm scared.

Again we find the playwright dealing with approaching middle-age, this time not in the area of sexual prowess, but in the matter of basic feelings of value and worth jeopardized by being forty-seven and facing the loss of a position after twenty-two years with the same company.

Edna suggests that if Mel does lose his job, they won't have much to give up, since they are living like "caged animals in a Second Avenue zoo" anyway, and sincerely asserts that she will go anywhere, do anything to help her husband feel better. He is very close to breaking down, when the serious tone is lightened by a phone call from the stewardesses who now complain about Mel's loud voice so that the scene closes with the girls banging on the Edisons' wall and Edna banging back at Mel's insistence. This is followed at once by a ridiculous news report done in the darkness by the voice of Roger Keating, whose final item is a notation that there has been a dramatic rise in the number of apartment house burglaries.

In the following scene, a few days later, the living room is in a shambles. It seems that Keating's statistic has now become reality for the Edisons. There are a great many laugh lines in this scene too, as Edna finally confesses that she had left the apartment door unlocked because she couldn't find her key and had gone to the store "for just five minutes." The burglars had taken all the usual items—TV, money, clothes—and also some unusual ones, such as mouthwash and dental floss, which gives Edna an opportunity to say that only *sick, sick, sick people* live in the world today. At this moment Mel confesses that this is really a very special day since he's been fired along with six other executives, twelve salesmen, and twenty-four office workers in a company move to "cut down expenses." He goes on to consider all the items he and Edna must do without, and in this section of the play Simon gets in some really heavy licks against consumerism as promoted by Madison Avenue. Mel says:

> The garbage! The garbage that we buy every year. Useless, meaningless garbage that fills up the house until you throw it out there and it becomes garbage again and stinks up the house. . . Two dollars' worth of food that comes in three dollars' worth of wrapping. Telephone calls to find out what time it is because you're too lazy to look at a clock. . . . The food we never ate, the books we never read, the records we never played. Look at this! Eight and a half dollars for a musical whiskey pourer. *Eight and a half dollars!* God forbid we should get a

little bored while we're pouring whiskey! Toys, toys, novelties, gimmicks, trivia, garbage, crap, *horseshit!*

As Mel warms to his subject, however, his voice becomes correspondingly louder and louder, and he is called to task this time by his neighbor upstairs who finally becomes so exasperated at the volume that he drenches Mel with a bucket of water thrown from his terrace. The scene and act end with Edna trying to console the now-sobbing Mel, revealing her depth of feeling for him as she says:

> You mustn't get sick and die because I don't want to live in this world without you. . . . I don't like it here! I don't want you to leave me alone here. . . We'll show them, Mel. . . . We'll show them all.

Six weeks have passed by the beginning of Act II, and Mel is now in the depths of a depressed state with a decided tendency toward paranoia. Edna has gotten a job and comes home at noon to share a lunch with her husband, but she understands rather quickly that far from cheering him, she is depressing him still farther by being the only wage-earner. It is here that Neil Simon might be accused by women libbers of being chauvinistic since he makes the tacit assumption that Mel would have this reaction. However, in defense, it is quite probable that a man like Mel *would* take this attitude, *would* feel even more worthless because of Edna working. Her first reaction to his cutting remarks is anger, but as their conversation goes on, she realizes that Mel is seriously ill. He begins to talk wildly about a "plot" to keep him from finding a job, and as he keeps talking, he makes less and less sense. Finally, she asks him who is behind this "plot" and he answers:

> . . . It is the human race! . . . It is the sudden, irrevocable deterioration of the spirit of Man. It is Man undermining himself, causing a self-willed, self-imposed, self-evident *self destruction.* That's who it is.

Although his ranting is meant to indicate the depth of his paranoia and is, of course, an absurdity, there is a great deal of

Prisoner of Second Avenue — Photo by Martha Swope
(Actors, left to right) Vincent Gardenia, Dena Dietrich,
Florence Stanley, Tresa Hughes

serious truth here. The playwright is expressing what many people feel about modern man with his over-dependence on gadgets, his determination to be a winner at any cost, his obliviousness to other men, and his genuine "deterioration of spirit."

In a typical "kick the cat" syndrome Mel now focuses on the water-tossing neighbor, promising hysterically to get revenge by burying him with snow as he enters the building. When winter comes, of course. Edna, recognizing the nature of his illness, calls for a doctor's appointment as the scene goes dark, and' we have another Voice of Roger Keating report, as exaggerated but as funny as the first. This newscast ends with the promise of "a filmed story of how twenty million rats survive under the city. But first, this message from Ultra-Brite toothpaste."

Unlike most of Neil Simon's plays, four additional characters are introduced in Act II, scene 2. They are Mel's three older sisters and his older brother, Harry. In some very subtle interchange we learn about these people and their relationship to Mel, who has always been "the baby of the family." For instance, we find that Harry feels that *he* was never babied, never shown affection from the time he was seven years old—presumably the time of Mel's birth. He says, "I was never kissed. . . . I didn't need kissing. The whole world kissed Mel. Look where he is today." What it comes down to is that Mel's siblings have recognized his "nervous breakdown," and are visiting "where they haven't been invited for nine years" to help their brother and his family financially. Harry suggests that each one contribute "X" number of dollars a week, and Simon gets some chuckles out of the discussion of just what "X" stands for in hard cash. Of course, they all want to help, but, on the other hand, they are reluctant to make any sacrifices to do so. Harry wants them to chip in to pay the doctor bills, but when he says that Mel must see the doctor five times a week and follows it with, "And we'll all see this thing through to the end whether it takes a week or a month or a year or even five years," he is greeted with stony silence from his sisters. One of the good ladies verbalizes for all of them: "We're all in agreement. Except when you mention things like five years. I don't see any sense in curing Mel and ending up in the poor-house." Harry agrees with, "Well, we obviously can't afford to let Mel be sick forever. We've got to put a time limit on it. What do we give him to get better? Six months?"

When Edna enters and finds Mel's family so willing to help, she is overwhelmed by their generosity, particularly as Harry offers to make up any deficit should the doctor bills run to twenty or twenty-five thousand dollars. She tells the group, however, that she will manage current expenses, including the doctor bills, but that she is worried about Mel's future. Therefore, she suggests that they loan him $25,000 as a down payment on a summer camp for children, a project in which he seems interested. This, naturally, they refuse to do. Edna then leaves the room in a huff, as Mel comes in from a walk in the park without even noticing his visitors. When he does greet them, he talks quite normally, but the sisters in particular act as though he's mentally unbalanced. If the audience is in any doubt about his stage of recovery, the playwright makes it very clear that Mel is making progress as he tells his brother, "You don't look well to me, Harry. You're working too hard. . . . Don't work so hard, Harry. You have to relax more." This brings us back to the Six O'Clock News, this time with Stan Jennings sitting in for Roger Keating "who has been beaten and mugged leaving the studio" on the previous night.

In the final scene of the play (Act II, scene 3) Mel is recovering rapidly, but Edna has lost her job because her firm has gone bankrupt. Now it is she who over-reacts to such inconveniences as not having water for a bath because the water has been turned off and no one can locate the super [janitor]. She tells Mel that she banged on the wall for him (when the stewardesses were obstreperous); now she wants him to bang for her. Again, in a very funny scene the playwright is making the point that highly rational people can be driven to ridiculous behavior by the frustrations of living in this prison. Finally, Mel persuades her to go into the bathroom and wait for the water to be turned back on, as Harry enters with $25,000 for Mel's camp in Vermont. We learn still more about Harry in this scene, so that he becomes a fully developed character. It seems that he has had a bad case of sibling rivalry for the past forty-seven years! He feels that Mel was always the "family favorite," an honor which Mel will happily transfer to him. After refusing Harry's loan, however, Mel offers to kiss his brother which only convinces the senior sibling that Mel has not recovered from his "nervous breakdown," whatever the doctor has said, and Harry makes a hasty exit.

Mel then begins to argue with Edna about having mentioned the proposed camp to his family and accuses her of having asked them for the loan, humiliating him. She counters by telling him that it was she who suffered the humiliation of the "Spanish Inquisition" during his family's visit, while he was taking a "nice tranquilized walk in the park." Their voices become louder and louder, eliciting the expected response from the woman upstairs. She threatens to have her husband repeat his water-throwing act as soon as he comes home. Edna taunts her with having no water, but as Mel goes out to apologize for his wife's loud voice, he is drenched again. As he says, "People like that always have water. . . . They save it so that people like us can always get it." We see, as Edna does, that Mel is now the calm one, able to cope much more maturely with anger-provoking incidents than his wife can. Nevertheless, he does take the snow shovel out of the closet as the snow begins to fall, which leaves the audience laughing loudly in anticipation of Mel's revenge as Roger Keating reports that there is a forecast for a record forty-three inches of snow promised.

This "revenge" is really just a joke, emphasized by having Mel and Edna strike a pose with the shovel, a "contemporary *American Gothic,*" à la Grant Wood. What Simon implies is that the frustration basic to being "prisoners" will remain for the Edisons and for us all, unless society makes a gigantic group effort to effect change. Moving to another place won't necessarily alter or ameliorate the situation, as we hear early in Act I when Mel and Edna are discussing leaving New York permanently and Mel says, ". . . Vermont maybe? You think it's all rolling hills and maple syrup? They have more people on welfare up there than they have pancakes." An escape won't help the inmates; what is needed is a world without prisons.

It was Molière who conceived of comedy's function as the means by which to correct men's vices, and, of course, society is made up of men and women so that it reflects collectively their individual behavior. However, in the aggregate, their inconsequential errors become magnified so that the total group (society) seems far more evil than the mere sum of its members' sins. At any rate, if Molière's statement that "It is a vigorous blow to vices to expose them to public laughter" can be taken literally, Neil Simon has scored a knockout in *Prisoner of Second Avenue.*

The Sunshine Boys

First presented at the Broadhurst Theatre, New York City, by Emanuel Azenberg and Eugene V. Wolsk, December 20, 1972.

Director: Alan Arkin

Setting: Kert Lundell

Lighting: Tharon Musser

Costumes: Albert Wolsky

CAST

Willie Clark........................Jack Albertson
Ben Silverman ....Lewis J. Stadlen
Al Lewis ....Sam Levine
Patient ....Joe Young
Eddie...............................John Batiste
Sketch Nurse.......................Lee Meredith
Registered Nurse ....Minnie Gentry

Number of Performances: 538

The Sunshine Boys — Photo by Martha Swope
(Actors, left to right) Sam Levine, Jack Albertson

The Sunshine Boys (1972)

This play is quite a departure from Neil Simon's other works in that the two protagonists are not youthful nor middle-aged, but in their seventies. To the casual observer, it may seem that the absent-mindedness, the cantankerousness, even the near-senility of these men are subjects for laughter, but to those who have had intimate contact with the aged, the play is poignant and extremely moving, for it deals with a problem usually ignored in our youth-oriented society: old age.

The plot is simple. Al Lewis and Willie Clark, who had worked together as a famous vaudeville team (The Sunshine Boys) for forty-three years, are persuaded by Willie's nephew, Ben Silverman, to resurrect one of their old sketches as part of a TV special on the golden age of comedy. Each man vehemently protests that he is against working with his former partner, since they haven't seen each other for the past eleven years—nor talked for twelve. Nevertheless, they finally get as far as a studio rehearsal, when Lewis walks out and Clark has a serious heart attack, after which their partnership can continue only at the Actors' Home where they will wait for their "final curtain."

These two characters are clowns who have outlived their heyday, partially because of changing entertainment styles, partially because of their clashing personalities. However, the point that the playwright makes is clear: no matter what the circumstances, human dignity is a paramount requirement for everyone, but it is not a need easy to fulfill when one is old, isolated and dependent.

When the play opens, Willie Clark is discovered in his one-room hotel "suite," planted in front of a TV which is just background noise for his intermittant dozing. His condition is established at once when he doesn't recognize the tea kettle's whistle for what it is and answers the telephone instead of turning off the stove. After he's tripped over the cord of the television and the set suddenly "dies," Willie first bangs it and then impatiently calls down to the desk for Sandy (apparently the bellboy and general fix-it man) to come up at once and make the necessary repairs. Almost immediately we get an inkling of this character's need for respect when he says, "No, not Willie. *Mr. Clark* to you, please." And when he's told to check the plug, presumably because this has happened many times before, he answers, "It's not the plug. It's something else. I'll fix it myself," then hangs up and says, "When he calls me Mr. Clark, then I'll tell him it was the plug."

At this point Ben arrives for his regular Wednesday afternoon visit, and, as always, the old man has so much trouble manipulating the latch that he believes he's locked in until his nephew reminds him to slide the bolt, not force it. The ensuing dialogue makes several facts very clear: Willie's memory is just about gone—he can't remember the names of Ben's children even while he's talking about them; his health isn't very good—he must eat low-sodium salt-free food and isn't supposed to smoke cigars; and he has only one interest in life—show business. For example, he checks the *Variety* brought in by Ben and finds that a certain Sol Burton has died. He comments, "I knew him very well. A terrible person. Mean, mean. He should rest in peace but he was a mean person. His best friends didn't like him." And then he makes a remark typical of elderly people who don't want to think about their own closeness to death, "Eighty-nine years old, went like that, *from nothing.*"

Simon gives us the impression that in spite of "getting chest pains on Wednesdays," when he visits Willie, Ben really likes his uncle and wants to help him to survive, but the younger man naturally becomes very frustrated by Willie's childish obstinacy, and he sums up his feelings this way:

> How can I laugh when I see you like this, Uncle Willie? You sit in your pajamas all day in a freezing apartment watching soap operas on a $35 television set that doesn't have a horizontal hold. . . . You never eat anything. You never go out because you don't know how to work the lock on the door. And you wonder why I worry?

In addition to the discomfort Ben feels about the hopelessness of Willie's situation, he is further bedeviled by the old fellow's insistence that if his nephew were a really *good* agent, he could get work for his uncle at least in television commercials. We soon learn why this is easier said than done when Ben says, "The word is out in the business that you can't remember the lines and they're simply not interested."

Willie's answer gets the expected laugh as he replies with perfect timing, "I couldn't remember lines? *I couldn't remember the lines?* I don't remember that." However, it is genuinely tragic that after fifty-seven years in show business, the veteran has come to this. Finally, after some humorous play on Willie's assertion that only words which contain the sound of "K" are funny, Ben comes out with the big surprise: he does have a job for Willie! C.B.S. TV is doing a Special on the history of comedy and The Sunshine Boys have been invited to appear at a $10,000 fee. But, of course, Willie must work with his ex-partner in order to do their classic vaudeville sketch, "The Doctor and the Tax Examination," and this he flatly refuses to do. When questioned, the old man stoutly asserts that he hates Al Lewis and that he has good reason. For openers, he cites two specific complaints. Lewis always gave him "the finger" which means that at every opportunity Al poked Willie in the chest to emphasize certain lines of dialogue. Furthermore, he also spat in Willie's face as often as "he could work it into the act." Puzzled, Ben asks why Willie had continued his partnership with Lewis for forty-three years in view of these shenanigans, and Willie's reply gives an insight into the uncommonly close relationship shared by these two men. He answers without hesitation:

> Because he was terrific. . . . There'll never be another one like him. Nobody could time a joke, nobody could say a line the way he said it. [*and significantly*] I knew what he was thinking, he knew what I was thinking. . . . One person, that's what we were. No, no. Al Lewis was the best, the *best!* You understand?

With his usual skill, Neil Simon follows this rather serious revelation with a joke, very much within the scope of the character, as Willie then says, "As an actor, no one could touch him. As a human being, no one *wanted* to touch him," but the point has been made that these two people had achieved an almost symbiotic state, so that when we discover Willie's real reason for rancor, we can see genuine motivation. It is then revealed that eleven years earlier the Sunshine Boys had appeared on the Ed Sullivan Show, and at the end of the performance Al had abruptly announced his "retirement" with no advance notice, which had left his partner without an act. As Willie sees it, "Don't forget, when he retired himself, he retired me too. . . . And God damn it, I wasn't ready yet." Psychologically, the old man's anger seems to bear a distinct relationship to the rage experienced by some marital partners when deprived of their mates by death, intensified in this instance by the fact that Al Lewis presumably had made the choice of his own free will.

Now Willie asserts that he won't take Al back because he (Willie) is a "single," which is very moving since we have already learned that he cannot function in that role. Ben assures his uncle that Al wants to do the act not for money, but for his grandchildren, who have never seen him, at the same time revealing circumstances of Lewis's life, which make it clear that his world is as empty and miserable as Willie's. He says that Al is now a widower, living with his married daughter and her family in New Jersey, with "very bad arthritis, asthma, and poor blood circulation." This gives Willie an opening for a joke about Lewis now using a cane instead of a finger to poke him with, but the playwright has made his point. Old age is a time of life distinctly different from the euphemistic "golden years" touted by those who sell real estate in retirement communities. It is a period during which ill health and decreased vitality may make one dependent as a child is dependent, but with a significant difference: there is nothing to look forward to except death.

Ben finally persuades his uncle to agree to a trial rehearsal, and the scene ends as the young man telephones Al Lewis to come to New York on the following Monday, as Willie prattles on about Al eschewing "juicy" words like Toy Telephones Tapping on Tin Turtles—or else.

On the day appointed for the meeting, which is scene 2, Ben arrives before Al Lewis and finds that although Willie now wears a suit jacket over his pajamas instead of his customary bathrobe—he's "half-dressed" as a concession to the occasion—the old man now tells his nephew that he has changed his mind about doing the show. It is noteworthy that in his effort to hold his uncle to his commitment, Ben addresses the elderly man as though he were a child, saying, "Behave yourself!" several times, an affront to Willie's dignity which does not go unnoticed.

At precisely two minutes past eleven Al Lewis knocks at the door, which is a signal to Willie Clark to leave the room and "make tea." Naturally, this means that Ben must play host and Simon takes advantage of the opportunity by creating some very humorous dialogue between the sophisticated young agent and the nearly senile Lewis. For instance:

BEN: er... did you have any trouble getting in from Jersey?
AL: My daughter drove me in. She has a car.
BEN: Oh. That's nice.
AL: A 1972 Chrysler— black.
BEN: Yes, the Chrysler's a wonderful car.
AL: The big one. . . The Imperial.
BEN: I know. I drove it.
AL: My daughter's car?
BEN: No. The big Chrysler Imperial. . . I rented one in California.
AL: No, she owns.
BEN: I understand. . . Do you come to New York often?
AL: Today's the first time in two years.
BEN: Really? Well, how did you find it?
AL: My daughter drove.

Since Willie remains out of sight, Ben must continue trying to make conversation, culminating in his making a prop list for the planned TV show, as dictated by the old timer. It seems that among other things they will need an "ahh stick," a "look stick," a three pound piece of liver (Al tells him, "A little laugh is a pound. A big laugh is two pounds. . . . Three pounds with a lot of blood'll bring the house down."), and a blond with specific and generous dimensions fore and aft—to play the nurse. It seems that Al knows just the person for this role, but she's now fifty-five or sixty years old! Ben finally escapes, leaving the two ex-partners to sip their tea with only oblique attempts at conversation. Neither man can resist the temptation to trade insults, however, so they are soon communicating at least on that level.

Al asserts that he likes the "quiet noises" of the country, and Willie pretends that he must remain in the city to be near the hub of theatrical activity for his work. But here and there, their basic needs show through the camouflage which makes the scene "play" on two levels: the obvious comic and the underlying tragic. For instance, when Al says, "I have a very nice room with my daughter in New Jersey. . . . I have my own bathroom. They don't bother me. I don't bother them," what he is expressing is his need for being "bothered," noticed, needed. And in the same way, when Willie says "I like a busy life. That's why I love the city," he is revealing his need to be involved as he is no longer and never will be again. Of course, neither man will admit his desire to do the sketch—Willie is doing it for his nephew's career, Al for his grandchildren—but they finally agree that although both of them are "against doing it," they will try to rehearse.

The two old men now arrange and rearrange the furniture and bicker comically and endlessly about the opening line. Shall it be "Come in," as Lewis suggests, or "Enter," as Clark demands in order to "freshen up the act"? Finally the bickering becomes a full-blown battle, so that when Al's daughter, Doris, telephones, her father is preparing to leave. This is no surprise, since Al, anticipating difficulties, had instructed her to make hourly calls throughout the afternoon. Willie takes over, telling her, "Unpleasantness? There was no unpleasantness. . . . There was stupidity maybe, but no unpleasantness," and comes away from the phone saying that he has promised *Dorothy* (he can't even remember her name, Doris, for the few minutes' telephone conversation!) that they'd give it one more chance. The act then ends with Willie yelling, "ENNN-TERRRR!" as Al screams, "LUNATIC BASTARD!"

The Sunshine Boys — Photo by Martha Swope
(Actors, left to right) Lee Meredith, Sam Levine, Jack Albertson

Somehow the Sunshine Boys have worked through their difficulties by the first scene of Act II, which takes place at C.B.S. where Ben is apologizing to the director for "technical problems" backstage which have held up rehearsals for the best part of a week. However, it is clear almost at once that these "problems" are personality-centered conflicts between the two partners, but, finally, the sketch is to get under way. Actually the scene is as much old-time burlesque as it is vaudeville because the two genres borrowed freely from each other in the era before burlesque became a term synonymous with nudity; therefore, much of the action and dialogue is mildly suggestive. Of course, in keeping with Willie's earlier lecture to Ben that the "K" sound is equal to comedy, the nurse's name is MacKintosh, the Tax Collector (played by Al Lewis) is Kornheiser, the Doctor (played by Willie Clark) is Klockmeyer, and a patient who calls to have her baby delivered is Mrs. Kolodny. The playwright makes excellent use of this opportunity to display at least part of this once popular theatrical form to those too young to have seen the original and to those old enough to remember the "good old days" with nostalgic longing. And it is very funny indeed.

However, as we would expect, nothing goes smoothly. Al gives Willie "the finger" and "spits" in his face. The dialogue turns into an exchange of personal insults, and finally, Lewis takes off his wig and jacket and leaves the studio. Willie then screams hysterically:

> I don't need you. I *never* needed you. You were nothing when I found you and that's what you are today. . . . He thinks I can't get work without him. . . . Maybe *his* career is over, but not mine. Maybe he's finished, but not me. You hear? NOT ME! NOT M—

with which he clutches at his chest and falls to the floor, an obvious victim of a heart attack.

After the lights dim, we hear the voice of the Announcer:

> . . . The golden age of comedy reached its zenith during a fabulous and glorious era known as Vaudeville. . . . Fanny Brice, W.C. Fields, Eddie Cantor, Ed Wynn, Will Rogers and a

host of other greats fill its Hall of Fame. There are two other names that belong on this list, but they can never be listed separately. . . They are more than a team. They are two comic shining lights that beam as one. . . For Lewis without Clark is like laughter without joy. . . . When these two greats retired, a comic style disappeared from the American scene that will never see its like again. . . . Here then in a sketch taped nearly eleven years ago on the Ed Sullivan Show, are Lewis and Clark in their classic scene, "The Doctor Will See You Now" . . .

and we hear the opening words of the sketch without knowing what has happened to Willie Clark. However, the play is a comedy, so the final scene gives us a "happy ending" although it doesn't come before Neil Simon has taken the opportunity to make further points in line with his theme: the vicissitudes of aging.

Two weeks have passed and Willie is now back in his hotel room, this time in bed, attended by a registered nurse, who happens to be a black woman. Here the playwright has created a minor character who is memorable in her own right, since she is entirely capable of "holding up her end" in the insult-joke game which her patient enjoys playing. Actually, both Nurse O'Neill and Willie seem to be having a fine time in their verbal skirmishes, providing a breather for the audience as well. When Ben arrives for his usual Wednesday visit, he brings *Variety* and about two hundred get-well telegrams from show business people. The room is filled with flowers, and the nurse has been munching on chocolates from a large box, so we may assume that Willie's seizure has gained some attention in his world of show business. Undoubtedly, this notice is pleasant for him; nevertheless, he remains as childishly peevish as ever. When Nurse O'Neill leaves for her lunch break, for example, she tells Willie that he must not get up to go to the bathroom, but must use "the you-know-what." Without even glancing up from *Variety*, he answers, "And if not, I'll do it you-know-where."

Almost at once Ben tries to talk to his uncle about a permanent retirement from the theatre, which is somewhat ironic since Willie has not been working for the past eleven

years! The old man, however, insists that he will make the
decision for himself, and finally Ben tells him:

> No, I decide for Willie Clark. I am your closest and *only* living
> relative and I am responsible for your welfare. . . . You can't
> live here anymore, Willie. Not alone, and I can't afford to keep
> this nurse on permanently. . . . We have to do something and
> we have to do it quickly.

What this amounts to, really, is that the younger man is "taking
over," not unkindly, but out of necessity. Still, the situation
causes a dependence relationship which certainly does not leave
much room for the older man to maintain his dignity. Ben then
goes on to tell Willie that he must move into his nephew's
home, into a "small spare room in the back," a plan which
Willie rejects jokingly, in keeping with his personality. He says,
"I don't like your kids. They're noisy. . . . No offense. But I'm
not living with your children. If you get rid of them, then we'll
talk."

Beneath the bantering tone, it is apparent that this elderly
man has had to come to terms with a terrifying fact: he will have
little choice as to how or where he will spend the rest of his life.
Ben thinks his desire to be independent is "stupid," and in fact,
the only alternative to living with his nephew's family is to move
to the Actors' Home. Ben means well, and he has investigated
this option by visiting the Home, but one remark of his, meant
to persuade his uncle that it is a desirable place, is quite telling.
He says:

> There's a million activities there. They put on shows every
> Friday and Saturday night. . . . I mean it's all old actors. What
> could be better for you? I couldn't get over how many old actors
> were there that I knew and remembered. *I thought they were
> all dead.* [Italics are mine]

Willie's reply is still "in character"—"Some recommendation. A house in the swamps with forgotten people," but when
he asks, "And what about you? . . . I won't see you no more?"
even the veteran clown must look away. Ben, of course,
promises to come and visit Willie every Wednesday and bring

Variety, but even Willie's quick, *"Don't bring the kids!* Why do you think I'm going to the home for?'' doesn't gloss over the basically tragic situation, for with very few exceptions most people who live long lives end either as "tolerated guests" in the homes of relatives or "paying guests" in old people's Homes. Here Neil Simon deftly avoids sentimentality by making use of the character's propensity to speak in one-liners, while at the same time making painfully clear the feeling of helplessness being experienced by this man, and, by extension, by all who find themselves in his position.

Ben now tells Willie that he'd like him to see his ex-partner, who has been heartsick over what's happened. Willie finally agrees, but is furious when he finds that Al Lewis is waiting in the hotel lobby. Again the pride and need for dignity come through as Willie says, "First you commit me to the Old Man's Home, bring that bastard here, and *then* you ask me." However, he will be an actor to the end, so he decides to make the most of the moment. He insists on getting out of bed, putting on his blue suit jacket, sitting on two pillows ("When I sit," he says, "I wanna look down on him."), and having his chair pushed all the way back, so Lewis will have a long walk. When Al knocks, he childishly answers with "En-terrrr!" and then immediately feigns sleep.

The situation is no better for Lewis. As he tiptoes in, he admits to Ben that he'd like to hold onto his hat—as a prop against nervousness—and is more than willing to leave at once since Willie is supposedly dozing. Ben "awakens" his uncle and then goes downstairs to get refreshments, leaving the two old men to talk—in the old insulting terms, naturally. Willie expects Al to formally apologize for having caused his heart attack. This his ex-partner has no intention of doing; he has only come to "say hello." A lot of very funny dialogue follows, eventually evolving into an old "joke" routine, which when recognized by both partners, makes them smile. Lewis reveals that his daughter is having another baby and so his room will be needed. Therefore, he tells Willie, he will be going to the Old Actors' Home. He says, "If you're not too busy, maybe you'll come over one day to the Actors' Home and visit me," but Willie, pretending to the end that he will be working soon, only replies, "You can count on it."

The play ends with Lewis and Clark involved in a pointless argument about a certain Bernie Eisenstein whose death has been reported in *Variety*. Was he the house doctor at the Palace or Rodriguez, of Ramona and Rodriguez? Even the "curtain call" for *The Sunshine Boys*, as provided in the script, has Al talking pointlessly about old times and forgotten people of the theatre, so that we know exactly how the two protagonists will spend what remains of their lives.

Of course, it is a fairy-tale ending, made necessary by the comic genre within which the playwright is working. The audience may comfortably leave the theatre, ignoring what will happen after the final bows, merely chuckling at the antics of these two old clowns. However, if looked at in another way, there is a pervasive sense of desperation here too, not because we must all experience a "final curtain" at the end of our play, but because so often there is no applause for actors who do not have the grace to quit the stage before they have grown old.

It may well be a coincidence that Neil Simon has given his characters the names of two men famed for their youthful feat of exploration, but, then again, it may have been done on purpose.

THE ODD COUPLE

THE SUNSHINE BOYS

THE GINGERBREAD LADY

PRISONER OF SECOND AVENUE

CALIFORNIA SUITE

CHAPTER TWO

The Good Doctor

First presented at the Eugene O'Neill Theatre, New York City, by Emanuel Azenberg and Eugene V. Wolsk, November 27, 1973.

Director: A. J. Antoon

Setting: Tony Walton

Lighting: Tharon Musser

Costumes: Tony Walton

Sound: Sandy Hacker

Musical Orchestrations: Peter Link

CAST

The Writer	Christopher Plummer
The Sneeze	Christopher Plummer, Rene Auberjonois, Marsha Mason, Barnard Hughes, Frances Sternhagen
The Governess	Frances Sternhagen, Marsha Mason
Surgery	Christopher Plummer, Barnard Hughes
Too Late for Happiness	Barnard Hughes, Frances Sternhagen
The Seduction	Christopher Plummer, Rene Auberjonois, Marsha Mason

The Drowned Man . . . . Christopher Plummer,
                    Rene Auberjonois, Barnard Hughes
The Audition . . . . Christopher Plummer,
                                      Marsha Mason
A Defenseless Creature . . . . Christopher Plummer,
                    Barnard Hughes, Frances Sternhagen
The Arrangement . . . . Christopher Plummer,
                    Rene Auberjonois, Marsha Mason
The Writer . . . . Christopher Plummer

Number of Performances: 208

The Good Doctor (1973)

This play is loosely based on some of Anton Chekhov's short
stories, interwoven with brief original sketches and bridges
between sketches by Neil Simon. This is really not a strange
collaboration, since "Doc" Simon and Anton Chekhov, M.D.
have a great deal in common, despite widely divergent origins.
Most significantly, these two authors share a view of the world
and the people in it: a comic view, if you will, which
encompasses great tolerance for the "fools these mortals be,"
and an attitude toward society which is somewhat critical, but
never carping. Both men seem to relish pure farce for its own
sake; both are capable of great seriousness as well. One
difference: Chekhov always considered his plays to be comedies
and wrangled with Constantin Stanislavsky who interpreted
them as serious dramas at the Moscow Art Theatre[1]; Neil
Simon's somewhat serious dramas are consistently interpreted
as comedies by commercial producers.

As originally presented, two women and three men play all
the roles, with one of the men doing both Narrator (and Writer)
and, at times, various characters within the sketches. In this
play this kind of casting is not only a boon to versatile
performers and a pleasure to the audience, but also a means of
achieving a strange kind of unity—as though they were all
figures woven into a tapestry portraying various facets of
Russian life in the late nineteenth century.

The evening begins with a concert—musicians on stage—
with seven short pieces giving the flavor of time and place. The
music (written by Peter Link with lyrics by Neil Simon) ends as
the musicians walk off stage and the Narrator (programmed as
the Writer) appears and talks directly to the audience,
humorously disclaiming his profession, but revealing, as Simon

The Good Doctor — Photo by Joseph Abeles Studio
(Actors, left to right) front row, Frances Sternhagen, Barnard
Hughes; back row, Christopher Plummer, Marsha Mason,
Rene Auberjonois

has elsewhere, his obsession for observation of all his fellow creatures in a mental notebook for future characters. At one point it is very difficult to tell if it is Chekhov or Simon who confides:

> I have no choice. I am a writer. While I'm writing, I enjoy it. And I like reading the proofs; but as soon as it appears in print, I can't bear it. I see that it's all wrong, a mistake, that it ought never to have been written, and I am miserable. . . . Then the public reads it: 'Yes, charming, clever . . . charming but a far cry from Tolstoy,' or 'A fine thing, but Turgenev's *Fathers and Sons* is better.' And so it will be to my dying day. . . . Charming and clever, charming and clever. Nothing more. And when I die my friends will walk by my grave and say, 'Here lies so and so, a good writer, but Turgenev was better.'

He continues to tell the audience a bit about himself, but just as The Writer is about to confess what he's really "always wanted to do with his life," he is sparked by the word "theatre" to tell another "story," one which is set in a theatre on opening night. It begins:

> With the arrival of all those dear and devoted patrons of the arts who wave and greet one another in the Grand Salon, commenting on how this one looks and how that one is dressed—scarcely knowing what play they are about to see that evening. [Sound like a Broadway first night?]

However, he goes on, there is one genuinely passionate theatre goer, a lowly clerk in the Ministry of Public Parks, who has splurged on good seats to see the play. He is Illyitch Cherdyakov and as he and his wife are seated, it is apparent that this evening is to be a high spot in their otherwise dull life. Little do they know just how "high" it will be! In this sketch called, "The Sneeze," these two good people find themselves seated just behind the Minister of Public Parks, General Mikail Brassilhov, Cherdyakov's supervisor. The General and his wife are totally uninterested in the introductions initiated by Cherdyakov, since the very existence of an "Assistant Clerk in the Department of Trees and Bushes" is outside their ken.

Finally, the group is "shushed" by the Narrator, and it seems that the audience can settle back to enjoy an unseen play, *The Bearded Countess*. Alas, the calm is shattered almost at once by Cherdyakov, who sneezes so monstrously that he wets the back of the General's neck and head. Almost apoplectic in his apology, the poor clerk cannot let the matter rest, continuing to replay the incident over and over in his mind. (This replaying is portrayed by repeated slow-motion dreamlike movements by the actors.) He tells his wife that he will be "fired from Trees and Bushes, sent down to Branches and Twigs," and he regrets not sitting in the balcony with "people of his own class, who love sneezing on each other." Almost desperately, the distraught clerk decides to visit the General the next day, and after waiting while the official receives "petitioners," he abjectly begs for forgiveness. As he puts it:

> I just wanted to point out there was no political or anti-social motivation behind my sneeze. It was a non-partisan, non-violent act of God. . . I curse the day the protruberance formed itself on my face. It's a hateful nose, Sir, and I am not responsible for its indiscretions. (*grabbing his nose*). Punish that which committed the crime, but absolve the innocent body behind it. Exile my nose, but forgive me, your Kindship.

Of course, this absurdity is very amusing. But this speech and all that follows is a cloaked criticism of the highly stratified society that Chekhov observed, and by implication, it is a negative judgment of all societies which accept the notion of stratification by "social classes."[2]

The General, who hasn't really thought about the sneeze at all, graciously "forgives" him, and Cherdyakov is very happy. He says, "I worship the chair you sit on and the uniform you wear that sits on the chair I worship." Oh, yes, he is happy— and yet—he begins to fancy that the General has toyed with him, humiliated him, made him grovel and beg, and reduced him (as he tells his wife) to a "gibbering idiot." The fact is that he has done these things to himself, but he doesn't realize this, and so decides to return to the General's office and "tell him what I think of him." He tells his wife:

The lower classes must speak up. . . . The world must be made
safe so that men of all nations and creeds, regardless of color or
religion, will be free to sneeze on their superiors!

When Cherdyakov gets to the General's office, however, that
haughty gentleman doesn't even recognize him and so is
understandably bewildered by the clerk's "revolutionary"
speech. In answer to the General's "What is it?" Cherdyakov
replies:

> What is it? What is it, you ask? You sit there behind your desk
> and ask, what is it? You sit there in your lofty position as
> General and Minister of Public Parks, a member in high
> standing among the upper class and ask me, a lowly civil
> servant, what is it? You sit there with full knowledge that there
> is no equality in this life, that there are those of us who serve
> and those that are served, those of us that obey and those that
> are obeyed, those of us who bow and those that are bowed to,
> that in this life certain events take place that cause some of us
> to be humiliated and those that are the cause of that
> humiliation . . . and still you ask *What is it?*

But when the General simply repeats his question, Cherdyakov
folds like a fan and begins again his abject apology for the
original sneeze, sneezing again, which completely infuriates the
General who then orders him out forever.

"Then," says the Narrator, "Something broke loose inside
of Cherdyakov . . . something so deep and vital, so organic, that
the damage that was done seemed irreparable. He then went
home, removed his coat, lay down on the sofa—and died."

After Cherdyakov has pantomimed this action and "died,"
there is a blackout, followed at once by a return of the Narrator,
who tells us:

> Wait! For those who are offended by life's cruelty, there is an
> alternate ending. . . . 'Ivan Illyitch Cherdyakov went home,
> took off his coat, lay down on the sofa . . . and inherited five
> million rubles.' There's not much point to it, but it is uplifting
> . . . I assure you it is not my intention to paint life any harsher
> than it is. . . . But some of us are indeed trapped. Witness the

predicament of a young governess who cares for and educates the children of a well-to-do family.

This speech leads into the next sketch, "The Governess."

In this two-person scene the Mistress starts out to pay the young Governess her wages, using every possible excuse to deduct rubles from what is owed. Finally, the forty rubles a month (reduced almost in the first speech to thirty as the Mistress refers to her non-existent account book) for two months is made to total only eleven rubles and even that is reduced to ten when the Mistress insists that she handed Julia eleven and she "must have dropped one on the floor."

The Governess is about to leave after thanking her Mistress for the ten rubles, which brings out the point of the piece. Her Mistress says:

> Don't you realize what I've done? I've cheated you, robbed you. I have no such notes in my book. I made up whatever came into my mind. Instead of the eighty rubles which I owe you, I gave you only ten. I have actually stolen from you and still you thank me. . . . Why?

Julia's reply, "In the other places I've worked, they didn't give me anything at all," doesn't satisfy the Mistress—nor quite obviously Chekhov. After giving Julia the full amount due—eighty rubles—the employer lectures the young lady and one feels that the author is speaking through the Mistress as she says:

> Is it possible to be so spineless? Why don't you protest? Why don't you speak up? Why don't you cry out against this cruel and unjust treatment? Is it really possible to be so guileless, so innocent, such a—pardon me for being so blunt—such a simpleton?

Julia answers, "Yes, M'am, it's possible," curtsies again and leaves as the lights fade.

As a bridge to the next sketch, "Surgery," which is pure farce, the Narrator comes on alone with:

> Wait! for those again who are offended by life's cruelty, there
> is an alternative ending. Julia was so enraged by such cruel and
> unjust treatment that she quit her job on the spot and went back
> to her poor parents—where she inherited five million rubles.

Then, almost confidentially, he tells the audience that Man is
the only living creature capable of laughter, which supposedly
separates him from the lower forms; however, there is
something to wonder at, since one may well ruminate about the
objects of that laughter: pain, for example.

The sketch itself is really a rehash of an old vaudeville
routine, picturing an "amateur dentist" pulling the tooth (or
attempting to pull the tooth) of a reluctant "patient." The scene
usually ends with either the wrong tooth having been extracted,
or, as this one does, with the "roots" still in the sufferer's
mouth and the two (practitioner and patient) locked in physical
combat. It is completely farcical, of course, but the point that
pain, providing it is someone else's pain, evokes laughter is a
truism clearly illustrated by the violence in animated cartoons,
funny even to small children. In the broader sense, this
tendency to laugh at pain can be said to be a building block of
much comic writing, including some of Neil Simon's plays, a
notion which will be treated in more detail in the concluding
chapter.

Scene 5, entitled "Too Late for Happiness" is an oddity,
since the two characters speak to one another, but sing their
inner thoughts to the audience. However, it does "work,"
theatrically speaking, if played unselfconsciously, with no
attempt to make more of it than it is. Two old people meet in the
park on a fall day; both are lonely and both consider the possibility of filling their lives by relating to each other. The
gentleman finally does invite the lady to tea and she accepts,
but then says, "But not today. It's getting late. . . . Perhaps
tomorrow." He agrees that "There's always tomorrow," and
they walk in opposite directions.

The implication is very clear. Since, as he has said, "Winter
is just beyond that tree," there is little chance that there will be
a "tomorrow," certainly not for both of them. The choice is
between remaining single and lonely or risking involvement

which can last only for a short time before death must bring loss
once again. The scene closes on their final song—sung by both
of them:

> Yes, there's still time for happiness
> Time to be gay
> Still time to answer yes—
> But just not today. . . .

Act I ends with the sixth sketch entitled "The Seduction." It
is a highly amusing and quite sophisticated piece, which illustrates the use of reverse psychology, first, as a technique
whereby a dashing young man assures the audience that he will
give them a "lesson" in how to seduce a young wife by using
her husband as the innocent go-between; and then showing how
the "almost seduced" wife uses it to avoid ruination.

The Narrator (Writer) becomes the would-be seducer and
stresses each point as it is "acted out," very much as a teacher
would do in a classroom or laboratory. First, he ignores the lady
when he meets the married couple in the park, telling the
husband that he's waiting to catch a glimpse of a married lady
with whom he's madly in love. Next, he piques the wife's
interest by telling the husband various tales about himself
which, of course, the husband guilelessly repeats to the wife.
Finally, he flatters the lady as her husband reports his remarks:
she should be an actress; she should be a model for a famous
artist, and so on. And at each step, the Narrator-Seducer
involves the audience by "asides" directed to them alone. For
example, at one point the husband tells his wife that his friend
has actually accused him of not understanding the lady. He
says, "The man is weird. Definitely weird." At which the
Seducer says to the audience:

> He's delivering my love letters, sealing them with kisses and
> calls *me* weird . . . I ask you! So—let's see what we've got so
> far. The poor woman is definitely consumed with a passion to
> meet me. She is sure I am the only man who truly understands
> her. Her yawning, disinterested husband transmits my remarks
> but it is my voice she hears, my words that sing in her heart.

> The sweet poison is doing its work. I am relentless. There is no
> room for mercy in the seducing business.

Finally, the husband tells his wife that his friend Peter is a
very lonely man: "He says he has no relatives, no true friends,
not a soul who understands him" a speech almost tailored to
putting the goal in sight for the Seducer, who then turns to the
audience, saying:

> Please, no applause. I couldn't have done it alone. I share that
> honor with my good friend and collaborator, her husband. He
> wooed her so successfully that there is no carriage fast enough
> for her to be in my arms. . . . She ran all the way. . . . Observe!

And, on cue, the wife appears. However, before Peter can take
her into his arms, she stops him and tells him that she knows
how he has used her husband as "a clever and devious device"
to arouse her passions, and goes on to explain that indeed his
plan has worked. If he wants her, she will be his. At the same
time, she tells him that she has an "even marriage" which he
might prefer to allow her to continue. The choice is to be
entirely his. The Seducer now looks straight at the audience, as
if asking for advice, and then tries to lift his arms to enfold his
beloved, but finds he cannot complete his plan, so the wife
escapes. At this point the Narrator (Writer) tells us that after
that day:

> Peter Semyonych, the *former* seducer of other men's wives,
> turned his attention to single, unmarried women only. . . . Until
> one day, the perfect girl came along, and the confirmed
> bachelor married at last. . . . He is a completely happy man . . .
> except possibly on those occasions when some dashing young
> officer tells him how attractive he finds his lovely young wife.

Following intermission, the first sketch in Act II, "The
Drowned Man" brings the Narrator onstage, this time
supposedly walking on a pier at the edge of a dock at dusk on a
chilly day. He begins by telling the audience that he is
experiencing a difficulty not uncommon among writers—a

block. He can't think, he says, of a single good idea, or at least
of one he hasn't used before. He has some fun with the idea of
calling on God for help—even for the "germ of an idea—It
doesn't have to be original." He says, "I'm very clever at
twisting things around." And then he shamefacedly admits to
asking God to commit plagiarism. He is about to go home to bed
when he is approached by a down-on-his-luck sailor who sidles
up to him like a procurer and asks if he would like "a bit of
entertainment." As it turns out, the ragged man is not offering
the usual kind of "good time," but instead asks the author if he
would like to witness a drowning. Of course, this is shocking to
the writer, but he is assured that it is all a "show" and that the
sailor is most adept at performing this trick. During the course
of the sketch the gentleman, supposing the man a lunatic, tells a
passing policeman that he has been offered this "entertainment" for three rubles. Instead of being concerned about the
unbalanced man, however, the officer merely points out that the
price is too high; the writer should not have to pay more than
sixty kopeks! He says, "Why, the other day, right over there,
fourteen men acted out an entire shipwreck for three rubles."
"Mad! The world's gone mad," thinks the author and then
proceeds to go with it by haggling with the sailor about the
price. Not unexpectedly, the punchline is right out of old-time
vaudeville again. Before the fellow makes his entrance into the
water, he tells the author that he cannot swim and relies on a
co-actor to fish him out. This fellow is waiting in a nearby bar,
and the sailor instructs the spectator to call out "POPNICHEF-
SKY!" before it's too late. The writer is so engrossed in
watching the "drowning sailor" that he cannot remember "that
fellow's name" at the crucial moment. Too bad!

   The only speech which may have importance comes early in
the sketch when the Writer is still shocked by the sailor's
proposition. He tells the man that he thinks the idea of a faked
suicide is disgusting, but the entertainer replies:

> You overlook the finer points of my profession. Look here, did
> you ever see a coal miner at the end of a day? Filth and grime
> all over his body. Soot up his nostrils and in his ears, black grit
> in his teeth. Disgusting. . . Or a barber who goes home at night

with the cuttings of other people's hair sticking to his hands. It
gets in his bread, in his soup, it's nauseating. . . . Do you know
where a surgeon puts his fingers? Every man who works
eventually touches something filthy.

On the whole, however, this sketch fits into the category of pure
farce and really nothing more.

The second sketch in the second half of *The Good Doctor* is
called "The Audition." It is a brief piece, transparently Simon
poking a bit of gentle fun at Chekhov, since he has the unseen
author-director auditioning actresses with the usual off-
handed "Don't call us; we'll call you" attitude. A young girl
appears and gives all the wrong answers to the standard
questions. She stumbles over her name; she's not sure exactly
how old she is—until she finds out what age part is being cast;
she has a cold and a temperature of 103°; and all of her stage
experience has been in Odessa, not Moscow. The unseen voice
advises her to "get more experience and take some aspirin,"
but the girl tells him that she has traveled for four days to get to
Moscow, that she has waited six months for this audition (and
three months before that to get on the six months list), and that
it would fulfill a lifelong wish if he would just hear her. She
finally appeals to him with:

Even if you did not employ me, just to read for you would be a
memory I would cherish for all of my life. If I may be so bold,
Sir, I think you are one of the greatest living authors in all of
Russia.

She then refers to the story "Death of a Government Clerk,"
which is "The Sneeze," as "tragically funny" in order to agree
with his assessment of it as a tragedy after she'd labeled it
"hilarious," and so the audience surmises that the playwright-
director is just intending to listen to her in order to get her to
leave. He asks her which character from *The Three Sisters* she
wishes to do. "All of them," she replies, "if you have time."
Somewhat sarcastically he says, "Why don't you read the entire
play while you're at it?" and is nonplussed as she begins to do
just that. Finally, they agree on the closing scene and the

actress begins on cue to read Masha, then Irina, and then Olga, each with great feeling. Her goal having been attained, she thanks the unseen author and leaves, but his voice, indicating wonder at her great talent, speaks the final line (*softly*), "Will someone go get her before she walks all the way back to Odessa."

The third sketch, "A Defenseless Creature" is, like the first, pure slapstick comedy. The official of a bank, Kistunov, is crippled with gout and enters on crutches with his one foot swathed in heavy bandages. Inadvertently, he allows his assistant to show a poor woman (the defenseless creature of the title) into his office. As it turns out, she demands money due her sick husband—money which it seems his former employer owes the poor man—and she wishes the bank official to give it to her at once. It becomes clear very soon that her husband was never employed by this institution and so her demand is completely ridiculous. But she is very persistent, and so, after a long recital of her family woes and a variety of tactics ranging from loud screams and curses to a direct assault on Kistunov and his gouty foot, the woman gets her way. The official orders his assistant to give her the money and be rid of her before he has a complete nervous breakdown. At this point she reverses the curses she has put on him, thanks him profusely, and then foils his strategy as she exits with:

> Oh, there's one other thing, Sir. I'll need a letter of recommendation so my husband can get another job. Don't bother yourself about it today. I'll be back in the morning.

This assertion drives Kistunov into a complete frenzy, so that as the lights dim, he begins to beat his own bandaged foot, screaming madly, "She's coming back! She's coming back!"

In the final scene of the play the Narrator (Writer) addresses the audience directly, supposedly to relate an experience of his own youth, when on his nineteenth birthday, his father had taken him to the Red Light District to initiate him into the mysteries of sex. Chekhov Senior prides himself on being a "liberal father," and finally makes contact with a prostitute who agrees to act as "teacher" for young Antonshka. When the father haggles over the price, there are some amusing lines, but basically, this sketch is neither hilarious nor serious. It's not a very strong piece. The father realizes that his little Antonshka will be "Anton the man" when he descends the steps from the prostitute's room, so he decides to delay the episode for another year. "There's plenty of time," he says to his son, as the two of them walk off into the night together.

The lights come up once more as the Narrator talks to the audience, telling them that he had great affection for his father, but more, that:

> With him, as with all the other characters I've shared with you tonight, I have a sense of betrayal. . . When I put down my pen at the end of a day's work, I cannot help but feel that I have robbed my friends of their precious life fluid. . . . What makes my conscience torment me even more is that I've had a wonderful time writing today. . . I stand here with a feeling of great peace and contentment. . . . Thank you for this visit. . . . Goodnight.

Then he cannot resist the "running gag," and continues:

> Wait! There's an alternative ending. . . . If you ever pass this way again, I hope you inherit five million rubles. Goodnight.

On the whole, the second act of *The Good Doctor* is the weaker of the two acts, which doesn't increase the total effectiveness of the play. There is an interesting parallelism between the two playwrights: Chekhov and Simon—but aside from clarifying this relationship, the play can be taken only as an amusing evening in the theatre, not as one of the major works of either man. There is fun with farce; there is some social critique; and there are some interesting characterizations. When compared with some of Neil Simon's other plays, however, *The Good Doctor* is not outstanding.

1. In Chekhov's opinion *The Cherry Orchard* was "a jolly comedy, a vaudeville, almost a farce." To his death he insisted that "the last act is gay and light." In one of his last letters he still complained: "Why do the advertisements always call my play a drama? Nemirovich-Danchenko and Stanislavsky see in it a meaning different from what I have intended."

2. Almost without exception, Russian writers from Tolstoy to Gogol, from Dostoyevsky to Turgenev criticized— even if obliquely— the rampant stratification of society, just as Chekhov did in this piece.

God's Favorite

First presented at the Eugene O'Neill Theatre, New York City, by Emanuel Azenberg and Eugene V. Wolsk, December 11, 1974.

Director: Michael Bennett

Setting: William Ritman

Lighting: Tharon Musser

Costumes: Joseph G. Aulisi

CAST

Joe Benjamin	Vincent Gardenia
Ben Benjamin	Lawrence John Moss
Sarah Benjamin	Laura Esterman
Rose Benjamin	Maria Karnilova
David Benjamin	Terry Kiser
Mady	Rosetta LeNoire
Morris	Nick LaTour
Sidney Lipton	Charles Nelson Reilly

Number of Performances: 119

God's Favorite — Photo by Sheldon Secunda
(Actors, left to right) (standing) Charles Nelson Reilly;
(seated) Vincent Gardenia

God's Favorite (1974)

There is undoubtedly potential for comedy in the story of Job, with God and the Devil disputing over the faith of a single mortal, and an all-powerful Deity taking the trouble to test that individual just to win an argument with Satan. However, in this version, Neil Simon's unique ability to be amusing while dealing with serious ideas remains sadly unrealized. The obvious fault lies in the characterization, since in this play we see caricatures, rather than the three-dimensional people typical of Simon's work. Since he has eliminated both God and the Devil, as used by Archibald MacLeish in his play *JB* (1958), and Job has no "friends" to mourn with him, the only conflict in the play occurs between Joe Benjamin (representing Job) and a character cleverly created by the playwright, Sidney Lipton (representing God's messenger). When Lipton is onstage, the play comes to life; at other times, it is bogged down by running gags and topical allusions. It is ironic that this Biblical tale, which should almost automatically attain universality by virtue of its age and source, fails to achieve that quality so consistently found in most of the other plays written by Neil Simon.

Characterization is central, of course, since the theme of Job's faith in his God is predicated on the proposition that before the torturous tests begin Job is not only a prosperous man, but also a happy one. He bends beneath the burdens laid on him by the Almighty, but never breaks, and is rewarded in the end by a God whose confidence in him has been justified. In *God's Favorite*, however, Joe Benjamin is extremely wealthy, but not particularly content, even before God begins to try his patience. This is no wonder since living with the "family" pictured in this play would be a torture in itself. There is Rose, his wife, a woman whose horizon ends at the edge of her jewel box. She combines gross materialism and childish näiveté so that she appears to be an avaricious Gracie Allen. There is David, the Benjamins' elder son, who behaves reprehensively with no motivation but to punish his over-indulgent father.[1] And there are the twins, Sarah and Benjamin, whose moronic behavior makes it seem unlikely that they have even the "combined IQ of 160" designated by the playwright. Sarah particularly is so absurd that even with all of her father's money and academic standards lowered in anticipation of a possible endowment, it is highly unlikely that any college would accept her; yet she is supposed to be a co-ed. Even the family's two servants, Mady and Morris, seem stereotypes left over from *Gone With the Wind.* And the protagonist himself loses stature by reciting verbatim—as though learned by rote—his rationale for faith in God, stressing only his rise from rags to riches, as though he were insensitive to all else. So only Sidney— supposedly a somewhat "other-worldly" character—comes through as preposterous but memorable.

As the play begins, a burglar alarm sounds in the darkened palatial Long Island home of the Benjamins. Joe and the twins investigate, with Joe finding a pair of steel-rimmed spectacles dropped outside in the snow as the only clue to the identity of the would-be intruder. Even in this opening segment the humor is based on a "running gag," Sarah's inability to keep her bathrobe closed, and her concomitant fear, expressed with more than a hint of hope, that the burglar is really a would-be rapist. They decide that the man must have jumped from a balcony, and when they hear a noise supposedly signaling his return, all three stand poised to attack, at which point Rose enters. She is described by the playwright as a *"walking Harry Winston's,"* covered with jewels even in her nightclothes, and oblivious to the situation, since she is wearing earplugs, which apparently keep her not only from hearing, but also from seeing her husband and children with raised arms holding vases with which to hit the intruder. After the family members have all retired, son David enters from the balcony, dressed in an expensive tuxedo jacket, paired with patched jeans and sneakers. He is drunk and exchanges "smart aleck" remarks with his father and the twins when they return to find that he is "the intruder." Then Mady and Morris come in and report that they have both seen a prowler outside the mansion, exiting when Joe dismisses them, with Mady's line, "It's gettin' dangerous around here. I don't like livin' in rich neighborhoods," which prompts David to say, "She's right, Dad. Why don't you buy us a nice poor neighborhood so we'd all feel safer?"

As Joe goes outside to try to find the would-be intruder, Rose re-enters, this time clutching her overflowing jewel box. She asserts that she will not be upset if they will just tell her what's going on and then promptly faints, recovering rapidly with, "My jewels!" After Joe has finally calmed his wife and the twins by making them repeat that whatever happens, it is God's will, he tries to talk to David, who refuses to go along with his father's analysis of the situation. Joe asks his son why he tries so hard to fail. As he puts it:

> Quick with a flippant answer. Fresh, disrespectful, unambitious, no interests, no principles, no beliefs, no scruples, a drunkard, a gambler, a playboy, a lover, a bum, a television watcher and a lousy guitar player. . . And what makes it so painful to me is that you're the smartest one in the family. Three college degrees, finished first in your class, and you didn't even show up for your senior year. So why do you throw it all away, David?

The young man replies that when he's sober he gets a "single vision," which means seeing "frightening things in this house . . . money, money, money, money, money, money, money, money," which prompts his father to assert that he wouldn't mind if the house went up in smoke tomorrow; it would be God's will. Joe then goes on to recite a rather lengthy account of his own experiences, beginning:

> There was a time in my life when the holes in my socks were so big you could put them on from either end. . . . I grew up in a tenement in New York. My mother, my father and eleven kids in one and a half rooms. We had two beds and a cot, you had to take a number off the wall to go to sleep. . .

and concluding with,

All I wanted for my wife and children was not to suffer the way I did as a child, not to be deprived of life's barest necessities. But such riches, such wealth? I never asked for it. I never needed it. But when I ask myself, 'Why so much? Why all this?' I hear the voice of my mother say, 'It's God's will.' I give half of what I have every year to charity, and the next year I make twice as much. . . .

David, of course, is totally unimpressed and retires, leaving Joe to pray, "It's enough already, dear Lord. Don't give me any more. . . Just David. Give me back my David. . . If it be Your will, dear God, that's all I ask! Amen." He is quite startled to find his "Amen" echoed at once, which brings on Sidney Lipton, who is so blind without his second pair of eyes that he doesn't even know whether it's light or not. After Joe returns his steel-rimmed glasses, he looks around the room admiringly as he says, "How often does a person like me get inside one of these big-time houses?" but then denies that he's an antique dealer or that he's come to see Joe on business. At this point he has some funny lines about movies (*Chinatown* and others), but unfortunately the humor here depends on topicality. He then goes on to deny being a salesman or a travel agent, and finally, when Joe has lost his patience (a joke in itself, of course) and is about to throw him out as a lunatic, the irrepressible Lipton initiates a game of "Hot and Cold" with Joe to see if Joe can guess "his mission." Finally, the messenger comes on with:

> Very well. Forgive me, my son. I have taken these extra-ordinary measures, this bizarre form, so that I might present myself to you in some acceptable dimension, for had I told you the truth straight of my identity, even I could not have given you the power to accept or comprehend. Yes, Joe—I am who you think I am!

Quite naturally, the overwhelmed Joe then believes that Sidney is God, to which Lipton replies:

> Who? . . . God? *God?* Is that what you thought? That I was going to say I was God? My God, that I never figured on. Nothing personal, but that's really crazy. Why? Do I look like

God? Would God wear a filthy Robert Hall raincoat and a pair
of leaky Hush Puppies? In the winter? Would God wear
glasses? I mean if anyone's going to have good eyes, it's going
to be God. He's the one who gave them out. . . No, Joe, I'm
sorry to disappoint you, but I'm not God.

Finally, he declares that although he is not God, he does
perform "certain services" for God, not that he's a "lousy kid
from Western Union," but that he is a messenger just the same.
When Joe asks where he comes from, Sidney admits that he
does not live in Eternal Paradise or any place like that; he lives
in Jackson Heights, Queens. This conversation continues until
finally, in order to convince Joe of his true identity, Sidney
shows him a big "G" emblazoned on his T-shirt and then
almost gives the game away when he lets it slip that his
message is from God, but involves "the one from downstairs,
Mr. Nasty, Bad, Bad Leroy Brown, Satan himself," as well.
Ultimately, Sidney reveals the whole story of the argument
between "the two grown Deities" and their wager. As
expected, Joe asserts that no matter what is done to torture
him, he will never renounce God. To make it binding, the two
men get down on their knees while Sidney reads the "official"
message aloud, and here there are touches which are hilarious.
For example, Sidney misreads Joseph's name as Joseph *Marvin*
Benjamin, and when Joe corrects him on the middle name, he
squints and says, *"Melvin*—right—Would you believe God has
such lousy handwriting?"

His errand completed, the messenger is about to make a
dash for his bus back to Jackson Heights when Joe says, "It
doesn't make sense. Why? Why should I, a man who has
believed in God all his life, suddenly renounce Him?" This
starts a short dialogue which ends when the scene ends. It is
worth repeating:

SIDNEY: *(in answer to Joe's question)*
               I take home a hundred thirty-seven dollars a week. If
               you want theological advice call Billy Graham.
JOE: I am the servant of God. He is my Maker. I fear Him
               and I love Him, but come hell or high water, I will
               never renounce Him.

SIDNEY: Can I be honest? You can count on the hell and high
water. Good luck, Joe. I know you've got what it
takes. And no matter what terrible things happen to
you, remember that God loves you!
JOE: And I love Him!
SIDNEY: But in case the romance falls apart, here's my
number. Renouncements are toll-free calls.

At this moment there is the sound of fire engines clanging in the
distance; Joe's factory has burned to the ground and since God
was his only insurance, this can be considered a catastrophe.
Sidney has the last word with: "That was your mistake. Even
God is with John Hancock. . . . So long, Joe."

The second scene takes place two weeks later, and from the
look of things all has been far from normal for the Benjamins.
Some of the furniture is gone; the heat has been turned off; and
we learn that there has not been too much to eat. However,
Sidney's phone call to Joe—a nightly ritual—has not resulted in
a renunciation, and Joe decides at this point to explain to the
other members of his household what has been happening. He
begins:

You may have heard it said before, to love God is not to
question God. We must accept God as we accept the air and the
sky, the earth and the sun. . . Have any of you stopped to think
why, after a lifetime of luxury and prosperity, we're suddenly
living in a house that is twelve degrees colder than it is outside?
Have you wondered why plumbers, electricians, supermarkets
have all turned their backs on us? Why a butcher that I have
personally kept in business for fifteen years by buying the
finest beef in the world sends over meat that three of our cats
walked away from? The answer is. . . These things are
happening because they are *meant* to happen. The truth is . . . I
am being tested! Tested for my courage and strength.

Rose's first concern is that Joe not make his explanation too
long because the frost is caking up her eyelashes. Then she asks
if all of these "tests" they've been going through are for "an
insurance policy." Joe finally tells them about Sidney's visit,
eliciting responses typical for each member of the group. Rose
asks if the messenger wasn't really from UNICEF and without

being the least bit sarcastic, says, "OHHHHHH! I see. . . We all have to suffer because God loves you so much. Oh, Joe, I'm so proud of you. You must be thrilled to death." David, disbelieving of course, suggests that the least they can do is offer some opposition. As he puts it:

> Well, at least let's stand up and fight *Him!* I mean, the Man's been pushing people around for twenty-five thousand years. I don't think we have to take any more crap from Him.

His father protests loudly that he will not have that kind of language in the house so David obliges with:

> Then how about *outside* the house? Hey, God, You want to test us? Here we are! You want us to show You what *we're* made of? Show us what You're made of! What about it . . . Big Fella, show us a little muscle!

This speech is followed at once by a clap of thunder and a flash of lightning from a bolt which narrowly misses David. More of the same show of God's power prompts Joe to order the family into the basement for safety, with David the first to obey. Rose leaves with a line, "If you get a chance, get my bracelets," but Joe remains to pray to God for forgiveness of David's blasphemy as Sidney Lipton enters, his raincoat smoldering. It seems he had been under a tree as David called down God's wrath. After some amusing interchange, Sidney tries to persuade Joe to sign an authorization for "a small ad—tiny little type like 'Doggies Lost' in the Sunday *New York Times*," admitting that he has renounced God. Joe, of course, refuses and his physical tortures begin, each announced in advance by Lipton. Starting from itching on the palms of his hands to the soles of his feet, Joe progresses from neuralgia to bursitis and tennis elbow, with hemorrhoids closing the act, as Sidney leaves with a reminder to Joe that "If it gets worse . . . you've got my number."

Act II opens with the servants on stage in the completely burned-down remains of the house, making remarks which somehow are too close to "formula" to be very funny. For example, Mady says, "Well, I tell you one thing—I ain't cleanin' up this mess," to which Morris replies, "Well, you got to look on the bright side, Mady—at least we only got one floor to do now." Their ensuing conversation serves as exposition and we learn that somehow the fire which destroyed the Benjamin mansion missed all the neighboring places, that Joe is in agony, and that David has run out on the family. Rose is still ridiculous, clearing the path of debris as her husband enters, and then worrying about the "look" of a fallen beam in a certain position in the room. At this point no one can touch Joe; his skin is so sensitive. He can barely talk through his swollen lips and he can't swallow. Mady and Morris pray for him and Rose says, "Joe, isn't that sweet? They're praying for you and it's their day off." The two servants then ask everyone to join in the prayer, but Rose decides that they have had enough hardship and urges Joe to renounce God and restore them to their former position. As she puts it, "Say it, Joe, say it, and we can all go to bed and watch some television. Please." He refuses, and Rose announces that "He's not nice, Joe. If you don't renounce Him, [meaning God] Joe, I'm going to renounce you!" She then gathers the brood and leaves with the line, "Why couldn't God have tested a young couple with a small apartment?" She and the twins are followed by a reluctant pair of servants after Joe has told them to go, since, as he says, "What does a suffering man living all alone in ashes need two in help for?"

Now Joe asks God what is next and is answered by a voice, supposedly the Lord's, telling him that the test is over, but that he must just say, "I renounce God." Of course, the impersonator is Sidney Lipton who is trying to trick Joe by speaking over a cordless mike from a vantage point behind the fireplace. Again, Joe refuses and says that he shall just wait to die, but Sidney informs him that that event is a long way off and proceeds to read aloud a list of "coming attractions" from a hernia through "a touch of gonorrhea" and "all this only on the left side of the body." Sidney then confesses that he's been fired and has pulled this last stunt in a vain attempt to save his job by "making the sale," so to speak. Joe tells him that "We must carry what burdens God gives us," but Sidney replies, "Sure. The poor carry their burdens and the rich have them delivered," and goes on to renounce God himself in a really funny speech:

> I give you up, God! Thanks for nothing. The *Devil* cares more about people. At least he entertains them. The *Exorcist* grossed over one hundred thirty million dollars—domestic! . . . Hey, God, You hear me? May You have the same lousy weather You give us every year, especially Labor Day weekend.

Joe is very disturbed by Sidney's renunciation and tries to reassure the unemployed messenger that "all will be well." He promises to write a letter of recommendation for Sidney and to put in a good word for him with God. Just as Lipton is about to leave for an interview with United Parcel, however, both men see a "burning bush," the significance of which doesn't escape them. As Lipton says, "He never makes house calls. But with you, who knows?" It turns out, however, that in the ray of light which appears, it is not the Lord but David, not "blind drunk," as usual, but really blind. Joe is finally infuriated at God and says:

> Is this Your work? Is this Your test of faith and love? You blind my first born son and still expect me to love You? Punish *me*, not him! Blind me, not my son. . . . Where is Your love? Your compassion? Your justice? *I am angry at you, God! Really, really angry!* And *still* I don't renounce You! How do You like *that*, God?

This outburst is followed by another bolt of lightning, another crack of thunder, and David's eyesight is restored. Joe then apologizes to God with: "I'm sorry I lost my temper—but after all I'm only human. You don't know what it's like. Try it sometime."

Rose now enters carrying two bags of food which she has won on a TV game show, with the assistance of Don Rickles. And as she is followed by Sarah, her coat unbuttoned à la bathrobe in the opening scene, still prating about a would-be rapist following her on the street, looking her "up and down, up and down," we know that all has returned to normalcy for the

Benjamins. The family exits to what's left of the kitchen, leaving David onstage alone to "clean up some of the mess." He then looks toward Heaven and says, "Okay, God. If you've got room for one more, count me in. I just wanted to thank you for sparing my father's life. That's all I wanted to say. . . . Amen." Not unexpectedly, his final word is echoed from offstage as the inventive messenger appears to make one last try for reinstatement on his job:

> Don't worry, it's not who you're thinking. . . . I wonder if I could talk to you for a minute, young man? Guess who's absolutely crazy about you?

And the curtain descends.

Generally, Neil Simon creates characters with whom his audience can empathize. Therefore, even when their behavior becomes outrageously exaggerated in the course of the play, they remain interesting. In *God's Favorite* it is Sidney who illustrates this talent of Simon's brilliantly. Here we have an insecure, insignificant "nine-to-fiver," as he calls himself, living almost on the verge of poverty. He has a nagging wife who doesn't believe that he is a messenger of God. He has such bad eyesight that he can't see his hand in front of his face without his specs. And, by the end of the play, he's one of the unemployed. He has a tendency toward "splitting headaches," a marvelous facility with words, and enough imagination to say that the Devil is "gorgeous in a pink suit" and resembles Robert Redford. But then he constantly escapes his humdrum world by going to the movies, so it is not too surprising that he sees other people (even the Devil) in terms of Hollywood personalities. In a sense, he resembles so many people familiar to all of us that we can accept his "unusual occupation" quite easily. As he puts it in the first scene when Joe challenges him: "If He can have servants, why can't He afford messengers? He's got cleaning people; I've seen them!" And in the second act, after David's use of the word "crap" has evoked the bolt of lightning which nearly burns Sidney's raincoat, it seems momentarily logical that he should dial about thirty numbers and then leave a message with God's answering service. Of course, little that he does or says would stand up under careful scrutiny, but there is enough which is completely recognizable to carry the audience through the trait magnification which is part of farce. Unfortunately, even Joe lacks this quality for the most part; the other family members never approach it.

It is a happy thought that Neil Simon's next play, *The California Suite* has, particularly in two of its playlets, some of the very best work that the playwright has done to date.

1. It is noteworthy that even in Simon's first play, *Come Blow Your Horn,* the elder son, a "bum" in his father's eyes, is given a hedonistic motivation which is credible. David, on the other hand, doesn't even enjoy his self-indulgence.

California Suite

First presented at the Ahmanson Theatre, Los Angeles, California, by Emanuel Azenberg and Robert Fryer (Managing Director of Ahmanson Theatre), as World Premiere, April 23, 1976. Then opened at the Eugene O'Neill Theatre, New York City, June 30, 1976.

Director: Gene Saks

Setting: William Ritman

Lighting: Tharon Musser

Costumes: Jane Greenwood

CAST

VISITOR FROM NEW YORK

Hannah Warren .... Tammy Grimes
William Warren .... George Grizzard

VISITORS FROM PHILADELPHIA

Marvin Michaels .... Jack Weston
Bunny .... Leslie Easterbrook
Millie Michaels .... Barbara Barrie

VISITORS FROM LONDON

Sidney Nichols .... George Grizzard
Diana Nichols .... Tammy Grimes

VISITORS FROM CHICAGO

Mort Hollender .... Jack Weston
Beth Hollender .... Barbara Barrie
Stu Franklyn .... George Grizzard
Gert Franklyn .... Tammy Grimes

Number of Performances: L.A. 51; N.Y. 445

California Suite (1976)

Nine years and six plays after *Plaza Suite*, Neil Simon opened this play in Los Angeles, where it was very successful, and then took it to New York, where it became a typical Broadway "hit." Obviously, it has a structure somewhat parallel to his earlier work, in that it also takes place in a posh hotel, this time in Beverly Hills, and is constructed on the premise that a single suite housing four sets of occupants in succession could be considered a viable setting for four stories. In this group of playlets, however, the playwright stresses farce in only two of the pieces, while dealing quite overtly with very serious problems in the other two. This is not to say that Simon deserts the comic mode; he is constant and faithful to his muse, but the humor is definitely subordinated to the examination of frustrating and tragic life situations in "Visitor from New York" and "Visitors from London," and even in the lighter pieces, he continues to deal with concerns of importance, such as friendship, family relationships, and marital infidelity. Once again, the characters are for the most part middle-class and middle-aged so that on the surface it would appear that their lives would reflect at least a modicum of self-satisfaction and tranquility. But again—as in the earlier plays—beneath the placid exteriors there is often tumult, antagonism, and rage. Frequently, the very "jokes" which elicit audience laughter become in reality scalpels which probe and reveal inner emotions, some of which are not only bloody but also diseased. In characteristic fashion, however, Neil Simon maintains great sympathy for all his people—and empathy with them; we can therefore identify with them even when we are merely amused. The format for *California Suite* calls for two playlets before one intermission, two following.

The first is
"Visitor from New York"

The humor in this piece depends almost entirely on the traditional rivalry which exists between New Yorkers and Angelenos, particularly the transplanted variety. Since there are great differences in the life styles common to American coastal extremities, the characters, Hannah and Bill Warren, can be looked upon as symbols of the locales, combining truth and exaggeration as stereotypes typically do. Further, they are also representative of many people who find that the separate lives they live after being divorced are never truly single lives, like it or not, because of the child they share. Still, as Simon has created them, these two remain unique individuals, locked in a do-or-die battle to mold the future of their teen-age daughter, and reluctantly recognizing the pain that will be involved, regardless of the outcome. With exceptional skill the playwright uses the witty, sophisticated dialogue, which is entirely "in character" for these two, to create his usual humorous effect, but more, he uses the same dialogue to suggest verbal masks worn by each character to protect him/her from a former friend, now turned bitter enemy. One feels that beneath these disguises both Hannah and Bill have faces deeply etched by pain, faces which neither dares uncover too often, even when only looking into a mirror.

As the scene opens, Hannah is nervously awaiting her ex-husband, Bill Warren, to discuss the return of their young daughter, Jenny, to her mother's custody in New York. Hedging her bets, Hannah orders both double Scotch and tea brought to the suite, and then talks briefly via long distance to Bob in New York. It is apparent from her conversation that she is talking to a very intimate friend who is privy to the situation and entirely supportive. At this point Bill enters, Hannah greets him with the announcement that he seems to have turned "into a young boy again . . . the sweetest young fourteen-year-old boy," and the battle is enjoined. Divorced for nine years, these two apparently take up effortlessly where they had left off—one wise-crack following the next—New York sophistication versus Los Angeles casualness. "Billy" now, William Warren has

"Visitor From New York" — Photo by Martha Swope
(Actors, left to right) Tammy Grimes, George Grizzard

become a thorough-going Southern Californian, complete with
tan, denim slacks, open shirt, and sneakers. He's lost ten
pounds, given up liquor and cigarettes, taken up jogging and
swimming, and plays "eight sets of tennis every weekend."
Hannah seems much amused by the changes he has made in his
life, including the omission of an analyst because he has "gone
sane." She gets in some well-deserved licks regarding local
housing and common camouflage. Billy says he has moved.
"From Hardy Canyon?" she asks. "Laurel. Laurel Canyon," he
replies, and then goes on to describe his new house just a block
north of Sunset Boulevard as "a small French farmhouse."
Hannah remarks that she had passed something coming in from
the airport which she had taken for a Moroccan villa—"Turned
out to be a Texaco station." She then tells him that she is still in
their old apartment, almost casually admits that she has had a
hysterectomy, and remarks at once that she has heard of his
"prostate problem." Bill then mentions her "new boyfriend,"
and we learn that Bob is her lover, a newspaper man on the
Washington Post, fifty-four, with a heart condition, asthma, and
a leaning toward alcoholism. Further, he also has "the second
best mind in the country since Adlai Stevenson."

The chit-chat which serves as exposition as well as cover-up
for the couple's real feelings continues as Billy says he is
"seeing a very nice girl," and Hannah asks where he is seeing
her to. It becomes increasingly apparent that these two bright
individuals—each charming and civilized if viewed as a distinct
entity—could easily revert to some modern version of canni-
balism when forced to share a common yoke. And it is equally
clear that their earlier clashes must have given them good cause
to decide on permanent separation. Hannah taunts Bill about
his second wife, a singer, from whom he is also divorced; and
she wants to know all about his present "girl friend," an actress
with an eleven year old son. Finally, Bill tells the sophisticate
from New York that she is bitter, snide and sarcastic, and he
accuses her of being so busy clocking off zingers that she never
has a chance of letting an honest emotion or thought get
through. Not undaunted, Hannah retorts:

And you're so *filled* with honest emotions, you fall in love every time someone sings a ballad. You're worse than a hopeless romantic, you're a *hopeful* one. You're the kind of a man who would end the world's famine problem by having them all eat out . . . preferably at a good Chinese restaurant.

Finally, the embattled pair get down to the subject at hand—their daughter, Jenny. The way Hannah puts it:

What have you done to her, Billy? She's changed. . . She used to come back to New York after the summers here taller and anxious to see her friends. Now she meditates and eats alfalfa.

Bill then explains that the girl would like to try life in California for a year; she's not happy in New York. He explains: "I grant you it's an exciting, vibrant, stimulating, fabulous city, but it is not Mecca. . . . It just smells like it." Of course, he's missed the point, as Hannah tells him:

The hell with New York. Or Boston or Washington or Philadelphia. I don't care where Jenny lives, but how. She's an intelligent girl with a good mind. Let it grow and prosper. But what the hell is she going to learn in a community that has valet parking just to pick up four bagels and the *Hollywood Reporter?*

Hannah, speaking vehemently and out of deep hurt, fear and anger, is actually expressing the view held by many Easterners that all of Southern California is one huge Disneyland or Universal Studio Tour—a plastic wasteland, where, as she puts it, everyone of means drives a brown Mercedes, where there is no individuality, only group mindlessness—no genuine intellectual soil, only green cement. Bill, realizing that at one time he had held these same opinions says, "No wonder no one spoke to me here for the first two years." At the same time, we can discern the father's underlying sense of values when he asks his ex-wife to show concern for their daughter by respecting her right to make a free choice. At this point also we become aware of the kind of relationship which exists between Hannah and Jenny, at least in Hannah's view:

> She thinks I'm a son-of-a-bitch. . . But she also thinks I'm a *funny* son-of-a-bitch. She loves me, but she doesn't like me. She's afraid of me. She's intimidated by me. She respects me but wouldn't want to become like me.

Bill translates Jenny's feelings differently, however. She has told her father that she feels stifled ". . . That the only time she can really breathe freely is when she's out here." We learn that although the girl usually spends only July and August in California with her father, she has come now in November, and without her mother's permission. Of course, there are the usual reasons for a typically rebellious seventeen-year-old to "run away" simply because she has had a disagreement with her mother. But, more significantly, what Bill says may be true. He suggests that Jenny may well be lonely, not neglected, just deeply lonely. In rebuttal Hannah gets nastier and nastier, finally prompting her ex-husband to say, "You know something, Hannah, I don't like you anymore." Almost too suddenly her mask crumbles as she replies, "It's okay. I'm not always fond of me either. What are we going to do, Billy? I want my daughter back. You're the only one who can help me."

Bill then realizes that for once Hannah is revealing herself as she is: vulnerable, unloved by *her* mother, afraid of committing herself too deeply, while at the same time longing for the happiness which she pretends is banal. But he really does not know how to help her. He offers to have her meet his actress friend; he suggests that she might take her vacation in winter and spend the time in California near Jenny; finally, he tells her that their daughter is downstairs in his car with her bags packed, that Hannah may make the decision and he'll tell the girl that it was a decision made by both of them. This sort of behavior is exactly what Hannah cannot handle. If he had continued to fight her on her "tough" level, she would probably have taken the girl back with her at whatever cost. As it stands, she decides to forfeit her rights and agrees to allow Jenny to remain with her father for six months.

Almost at once, she begins to cover her nakedness with more smart repartee as in the beginning, making remarks such as: "I don't think you're prepared to take on your own daughter. Watching her swim for eight weeks at the beach is not the same as being a parent." And "Don't look now, Billy, but you just lost your sun tan. I love it. Oh, God, how I love it. Wait'll you see how she eats in winter. You'll be dead broke by Christmas." But when she refuses Billy's offer to say goodbye to Jenny, it is clear that she is close to breaking down. The nearest she comes is her remark, "I suddenly feel like an artist selling a painting he doesn't want to part with," as Billy hastily kisses her cheek and exits, leaving Hannah at the telephone complaining to room service, "I never got my God damned drinks!"

"Visitors from Philadelphia"

This second playlet is less realistic and closer to out and out farce (in the manner of Feydeau) than the first, since the visual or "sight gag" central to its humor is "onstage" from the beginning. Marvin Michaels, forty-two, wakes up in the darkened bedroom of the suite, plainly hung-over. He quickly discovers that since he had failed to leave a wake-up call with the hotel operator, it is too late to meet his wife's plane, that there is an empty bottle of vodka on the floor, and that there is a sleeping "hooker" in his bed! The girl is literally unconscious, and nothing the almost-hysterical Marvin can do to rouse her succeeds. Almost at once Millie Michaels arrives, upset with her husband because he had not met the plane, distraught because her luggage has been lost enroute, and on edge because she has just gotten "her period."

The next fifteen minutes are hilariously occupied with Marvin trying every ruse possible to keep his wife out of the bedroom. He tells her he's been sick all over the bathroom; he tries to send her out for medicine; he offers to take her shopping at once to replace the lost clothing before they must go to his

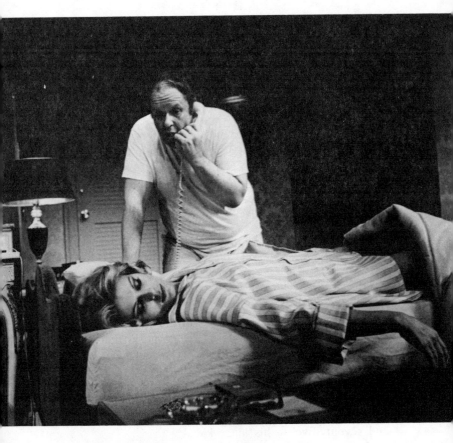

"Visitor from Philadelphia" — Photo by Steven Keull
(Actors, left to right) Leslie Easterbrook, Jack Weston

nephew's Bar Mitzvah. Nothing works and finally Marvin is reduced to confession.

It seems that the Michaels had decided to travel separately because of their two children, to avoid the possibility of their both being in the same airplane accident. And so on his first night in Los Angeles Marvin had had dinner and some drinks with his brother's family. When his brother had mentioned a present for Marvin "back at the hotel," Marvin had expected to find "a bowl of fruit maybe." Instead he had found this girl and that is all he remembers. As he describes it:

> Certainly I could have said no, but I didn't. She was in the room, she was attractive, she was a little tight, and she was paid for. And besides, I didn't want to insult Harry. He did it out of love. It's not much of an excuse. It will never happen again because not only did I not enjoy it, I don't even remember it! If you want to leave me, I would understand. . . . And when I kill myself, I hope *you* understand.

Millie, of course, is furious, but Simon keeps the zingers going even then. For example, she suggests that her errant husband take a picture of the three of them as a momento of her first trip to California. No camera? Perhaps they could call the official Bar Mitzvah photographer. She then asks what Marvin thinks the girl cost, and agreeing that it was about $50, counters with, "What a cheap brother you've got. We spent a hundred and seventy-five on his lousy kid."

It is obvious that in fifteen years of marriage Marvin has never before strayed and is genuinely contrite. He even offers to return to Philadelphia at once and skip the event for which they had come to Los Angeles. But Millie forgives him and decides that she will go to the affair, holding her head very high in the expensive new clothes she plans to buy in Beverly Hills. Marvin is delighted and the playlet ends as Millie sits on the bed to answer a telephone call from their children, with the hooker's arm flopping over her, crying as she tells the child:

> I do sound funny? Well, to tell the truth, I am a little upset, darling. . . . The airplane lost my luggage . . . the new dress I

bought for the Bar Mitzvah, my new shoes, everything. I am so
upset, darling. . . (the stage directions read: *her tears and the
curtain fall*).

Obviously, this is a frothy piece and the playwright keeps
the script brief, never overdoing the joke. It is highly unlikely
that the girl wouldn't wake up as Marvin tries to get her out into
the hall or stuff her into the closet, but like all good farce, the
nonsense is rooted in possibility (if not probability) and then
played "straight." With his typical tolerance for human
behavior and misbehavior, Simon makes us agree that one
transgression, particularly one which could be called a "sin of
omission," rather than a "sin of commission," should not ruin
what appears to be a reasonably happy marriage of fifteen years
duration. However, he does take a sly dig at Harry, the unseen
brother, who arranged for the "gift" in reciprocation for a girl
Marvin had "given" to him for his sixteenth birthday many
years earlier. Somehow the implication is there that Harry is not
quite so innocent and trustworthy as his brother from the "City
of Brotherly Love," Philadelphia.

The third playlet, which follows the single intermission,
reverts to the tone of the first in terms of style and the seriousness of its subject matter.

"Visitors from London"

It is now April and the late afternoon sunlight fills the suite
as the two occupants prepare to attend the Academy Awards
banquet. Diana Nichols, an English actress, has been
nominated for Best Actress and has come to Los Angeles with
her husband, Sidney, and high hopes of winning an Oscar. Joe
Levine and the studio have underwritten their entire trip down
to Diana's expensive gown and the flowers which fill the room,
so by rights these two visitors should be enjoying themselves
immensely, and to some extent they are. Diana, however, is
understandably nervous, and Sidney is trying very hard to calm

"Visitors From London" — Photo by Steven Keull
(Actors, left to right) George Grizzard, Tammy Grimes

her by means of what is apparently their normal mode of communication—sharp, witty, high-comedy repartee—the kind of verbal exchange usually connected with characters created by Noel Coward. For example, Diana is unhappy with her dress: she thinks it gives her a "hump" on the left shoulder, and when she complains, Sidney answers, "Use it, Sweetheart. People will pity you for your deformity and you're sure to win." Almost at once she tells him that she doesn't have a "sentimental reason" for the members of the Academy to vote for her, and suggests that "a dying husband would have insured everything," to which he retorts that if she had only told him sooner, he'd have come over on the Hindenburg. From time to time, through their chit-chat which is very brittle and very funny, Simon inserts some subtle foreshadowings which presage startling character revelations later in the piece, but which at the time seem only like lines from a sophisticated drawing-room comedy. It is noteworthy here that these are like clues in a well-written mystery; they don't come clear until the denouement when all the pieces fall into place quite naturally.

For instance, we learn that Sidney is an antique dealer who at one time had been an actor. When Diana suggests that he never should have given up acting and tells him, "You were so gentle on the stage. So unselfish, so giving. You had a sweet, gentle quality," he counters with, "Yes. I would have made a wonderful Ophelia. Pity I couldn't have stayed sixteen forever. What a future I had! Juliet, Roxanne, there were no end to the roles." And further on, Diana keeps asking why he's never in his shop afternoons, to which he replies, "There are no afternoons in London." It's all very light and frothy, but as they are about to leave the suite, Sidney gets quite serious. He tells his wife:

> I wish you everything. I wish you luck. I wish you love. I wish you happiness. You're a gifted and remarkable woman. You've put up with me and my shenanigans for twelve harrowing years and I don't know why. But I'm grateful. . . . You've had half a husband and three-quarters of a career. You deserve the full amount of everything. I hope you win the bloody Oscar. [Then, in an attempt at regaining his usual tone] Fifty years from now I'll be able to sell it for a fortune.

She answers, "I love you, Sidney," with complete sincerity, and then as her parrying thrust, Diana exits rehearsing her acceptance speech: "Ladies and gentlemen of the Academy, I thank you for this award. I have a lump in my throat and a hump in my dress."

After they've left, the stage is darkened to indicate the passage of time, and when the Nichols return to their suite at about two o'clock the next morning, they are quite drunk and in the foul mood to be expected since, of course, Diana has won no Oscar.

She begins to regale him by insisting that they are in the wrong suite, that they belong across the hall. Next, we learn that she has behaved obnoxiously ever since "Miss Big Boobs" went up to claim the Award for Best Actress. From their verbal exchange which is now only amusing in a bitter way, it is apparent that the evening has gone very badly for the couple, and that it would be wise if they were to go to sleep without any really serious discussions. Diana, however, against Sidney's better judgment, insists on a gut-level conversation and asks him about the "gorgeous" young actor with whom he'd shared a butter plate. He warns his wife not to get "into shallow waters," but she becomes more and more abusive, with a remark designed not just to make points, but to wound him deeply. She says:

> Adam, wasn't that his name? Adam, the first man . . . not very appropriate for you, is it? He did look very Californian, I thought. Sort of a ballsy Doris Day.

As they continue to talk, it becomes clear that Sidney is a practicing homosexual, in addition to being a sometime husband to Diana. She finally stoops to calling him a "faggot," just as he reminds her that she "does everything in her dressing room but dress," and we see that it is just because she loves her husband so much that Diana feels unbearably frustrated. He protests that he does "love her," as he puts it, more than any other woman he's ever met, and he asks her to remember that they have a good relationship in every other way. When she says that they've been "fighting this for years," and asks him,

"Why haven't I left you for a hairier person?" he gives her the only answer possible: "Because we do like each other . . . and we are each a refuge for our disappointments out there."

There is no need to point out that the playwright is dealing here with a very serious problem, not just in regard to sexual preferences, but more generally in regard to relationships among men and women, supportive and destructive, positive and tragic, but above all, widely divergent. And then, Simon doesn't close the playlet by simply implying that Diana and Sidney can continue as they are; he goes one step farther when at the very end Sidney kisses his wife very warmly, but with closed eyes, and she says, "Not tonight. . . *Look* at *me* tonight. Let it be *me* tonight." The lights then fade to complete darkness, not simply to fulfill the conventional signal for bringing down the curtain, but really to symbolize the incontrovertible fact that each of us is always alone at the core of our being, although we keep trying to avoid that condition by making whatever "connections" we can with other equally solitary human beings. And we do what we can to make these relationships work.

The final playlet in *California Suite* reverts to farce with a vengeance, as it is the Fourth of July at the Beverly Wilshire Hotel—and there are fireworks.

"Visitors from Chicago"

The first three playlets have two characters each (if we discount the "hooker" in "Philadelphia"), but in this final scene Simon uses two couples, first bringing on the Hollenders, Mort and Beth, soon followed by their friends, the Franklyns, Stu and Gert. These four very good friends have been on a three-week vacation together, with Los Angeles their last stop enroute home. We soon see that it has not really been much of a holiday, since the two men especially have very nearly come to the point of "telling each other off," so that almost any excuse will serve as the match with which to light the fuse on the fire-

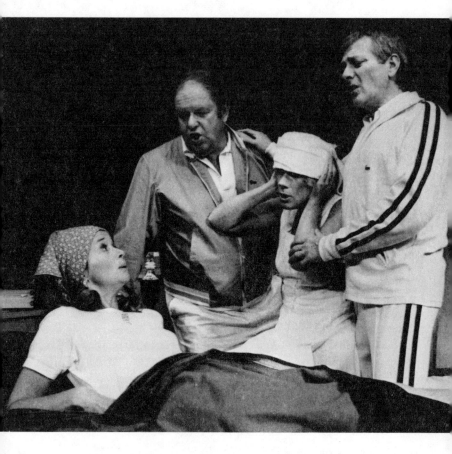

"Visitors from Chicago" — Photo by Steven Keull
(Actors, left to right) Barbara Barrie, Jack Weston, Tammy
Grimes, George Grizzard

cracker. When we first see Beth Hollender, she is being half-dragged, half-carried into the suite by her husband, who is loudly declaring his feelings about the Franklyns as he enters. Beth is in terrific pain with what may be a broken ankle, caused, her husband feels, by the way their friends insisted on playing tennis as though it were war: lobbing the ball at Beth when her shoe laces were untied and the sun was shining into her eyes!

Simon gets a lot of mileage out of jokes about calling a doctor from among those listed in the phone book: "It's Beverly Hills—you might get a psychiatrist," and from ordering enough ice for four people, but "No drinks, please, just ice" (to put on Beth's ankle, of course). But the real tone of the piece is set when Mort answers the telephone to talk to his "friend," Stu Franklyn. He says:

> How is she? How do you think she is? Her foot may be broken, that's how she is. It's the size of a cocoanut. . . . What can you do? I'll tell you what you can do. I want you to go to the proshop and buy two cans of yellow tennis balls, charge them to me, and shove them up your respective asses.

Beth, of course, protests, "Are you crazy? Those are our best friends," to which Mort answers, "I said I'd pay for the balls, didn't I?"

A few minutes later the Franklyns appear in person and the recriminations continue, not just about the tennis game, but about many other irritations and petty gripes each couple has until this point kept unvented. Each charge and counter-charge for the next fifteen minutes is punctuated hilariously by accidents, eventually involving the three who are not already on the disabled list—and culminating in the two injured wives side by side on the bed watching the two husbands engage in physical confrontation. Finally, all is bedlam.

Throughout the piece we catch glimpses of reality, character wise, but on the whole, the playlet depends on visual type humor for its effect. At the end, Stu has kicked Mort in the groin and bitten his leg as well; still, in the final skirmish, Mort, who is the heavier of the two men, has Stu in a strangle-hold and demands that Stu repeat after him that the vacation was splendid, which Stu must do since he is choking, and then that they will take their vacations together again next year, which Stu refuses to do, choking or not!

Anyone who has taken a vacation with friends can easily understand the basic premise: constant contact can lead to unexpected personality conflicts over sheer trivialities. And the playwright has exaggerated all these areas of dissension for purely comic effect. "Visitors from Chicago," then, lends a very upbeat ending to the total play, but it can qualify only as slapstick, pure and simple, not much else.

Seen as a total evening in the theatre, the characters in the four playlets have less obvious relationship to each other than the characters in *Plaza Suite*, except for those in the completely comic pieces: Millie Michaels has two "sisters" in Beth Hollender and Gert Franklyn; Marvin Michaels is not too different from Mort Hollender and Stu Franklyn. Any one of them might substitute for any other: middle-class, predictable, quite competitive, and a bit hypocritical. They are all "nice," in the sense that none of them will be caught stealing (although the men might be a bit "sharp" in their business practice); none of them will commit a murder (although Millie Michaels would like to "kill" Marvin's brother, Harry); and all of them would jump at the chance to attend the Academy Awards, happy that a "foreigner" did not win the Oscar for Best Actress.

In the first and third playlets, however, Neil Simon has capsulated and distilled relationships which are somewhat less common, but so "real" that they border on the tragic. In both "Visitor from New York" and "Visitors from London" we see people who show one set of faces to outsiders, another to each other. The common denominator is that all four of these characters (with the possible exception of Bill Warren) are people so deeply scarred that they have difficulty facing the truth about themselves, and instead cover up with sophisticated banter, truly terrified that confrontation with undeniable facts about themselves would be unbearable. Hannah Warren, Diana Nichols, and her husband, Sidney, are all attempting to cope as best they can with almost insupportable situations: Hannah with her "lost" child and her dying lover, the Nichols with

Sidney's Janus-like sexual orientation. But all have a certain gallantry, pluckiness, and resilience which we must admire, even as we see their flaws. The playwright has drawn these people with such verisimilitude that one feels that each has potential as a "character" who could go on to another Neil Simon play.

Chapter Two

First presented at the Ahmanson Theatre, Los Angeles, California, by Emanuel Azenberg and Robert Fryer (Managing Director of Ahmanson Theatre) as world première, October 7, 1977. It then opened at the Imperial Theatre, New York City, December 4, 1977.

Director: Herbert Ross

Setting: William Ritman

Lighting: Tharon Musser

Costumes: Noel Taylor

CAST

Jennie Malone.............................. Anita Gillette
Faye Medwick .... Ann Wedgeworth
George Schneider .... Judd Hirsch
Leo Schneider .... Cliff Gorman

Number of Performances: As of March, 1979, the play was still running.

Chapter Two (1977)

Neil Simon has stated that *Chapter Two* is the most autobiographical and the most painful play he has ever written. It is painful from the standpoint of the playwright who has attempted in it to objectify for his audience a very subjective loss—the untimely death of his first wife—and his feelings about making a commitment to continue his life in a second marriage. In the sense that most writers of fiction (including drama) create out of their own experiences, all of the genre may be considered somewhat autobiographical. At the same time, the very process of artistic selection involved in writing a play necessitates a departure from the absolute and complete "truth."

In this play Simon makes public the overwhelming grief he felt when Joan Simon died and the reluctant joy he accepted when he married Marsha Mason. The protagonist, George Schneider, who represents the playwright, feels that it is not possible to experience two such completely fulfilling relationships in only one life, and this reaction is very understandable. It is as though one were to win the grand prize in the Irish Sweepstakes two years in succession! Along with the conviction that no one *could* be so fortunate, there are also guilt feelings, as though being happy in a second relationship were somehow a betrayal of the first. Although biographically oriented criticism has some value in helping to illuminate any piece of work, in the final analysis *Chapter Two* must stand or fall on its own merits as a play, completely apart from any connection to the author's life.

The issue, then, in terms of the thesis of this study is whether or not *Chapter Two,* through characterization, clarifies a theme of universal importance. And it does.

It remains a comedy in spite of its subject because of Simon's usual facility with bright, witty dialogue, and, of course, its happy ending. It does, however, depart from the playwright's usual mode in that it has a sub-plot, loosely based on the characters of the protagonist's brother and a woman friend of the female lead. In one way, this additional story is effectively juxtaposed to the main plot, for these people, Leo Schneider and Faye Medwick, live their lives on a rather shallow level compared to George Schneider and Jennie Malone, never attaining more than transitory pleasure, and not too much of that. In another light, however, their presence detracts somewhat from the main thrust of the play, since at times it seems somewhat forced, almost as though the playwright were using it to cover up certain aspects of the central theme by purporting to deal with this second couple. In any case, the basic idea of *Chapter Two,* aside from the avowed connection to Simon's life, once again has universal application. Simply stated, the playwright is saying that one must accept a continuing connection to life even in the face of tragedy, and assume that commitment without self-pity or guilt, but with responsibility to and respect for those who stand ready to make life worth the living.

As the play opens, George Schneider has just come back to New York from a trip to Europe, taken to assuage his depression after his wife's death. His brother, Leo, well aware of George's continuing melancholy, tries at once to coax him into a return to "normal" daily living, with jokes about icicles in the bathroom because the shower had been dripping and the window left open, making it look like "the john in Dr. Zhivago," "white bread that's turned into pumpernickel all by itself," and a letter from Aunt (?) Henry. George, however, ignores these attempts at levity and instead reads aloud a letter of condolence written to him by his late wife's beautician. This little note epitomizes for him the sweet, empathetic nature of the woman who has died, and sets his mood for the audience as well. He then asserts that he never should have gone to the places once shared with his beloved Barbara; the memories had only made his loss less bearable. He says that he had expected to see her at every turn, a case of wishful thinking, and that finally he had come to the point of cursing her for having left him, a very common reaction to bereavement. He concludes now that Chapter Two in the life of George Schneider must begin. But where? Leo suggests all the usual divertisements: poker, a Knicks game, dinner—and shows his genuine sympathy for his brother, saying, as he embraces George with tears in his eyes, "Now I'm mad. I think it stinks too...I'm not going to forgive her for a long time." George then leaves the stage with, "Okay, let's take it one night at a time, folks," to end the first scene.

The stage setting is particularly noteworthy in *Chapter Two,* as the apartments of both its leading characters are fully visible to the audience at all times, a fact that serves several purposes. First, as the lights dim on George Schneider's apartment, they come up on Jennie Malone's, smoothing the transition between scenes. And more importantly, each apartment mutely represents the lifestyle of its occupant, so that where there is contrast, it becomes obvious at once. For example, as scene 2 opens, about two months later in Jennie's apartment, she too is returning from a trip, accompanied by her close friend, Faye. And Jennie too is depressed, returning to New York after having obtained a Mexican divorce. But the heat in the apartment has been turned on, and there is fresh food in the refrigerator because in her very organized fashion she has planned ahead. As she puts it, "It's that Catholic upbringing. I majored in discipline." Faye's character, like Leo's in the first scene, is exposed at once, as she reveals she and her husband, Sidney, have been having marital problems, apparently of an ongoing nature. Jennie is angry at the six years of her life which she feels have gone for naught, married to the pro-football player, Gus, and so she, like George, although for a very different reason, is determined to begin her Chapter Two very much alone.

In scene 3 we see George Schneider, novelist, trying without much success to work at his typewriter, and with his customary skill Simon lightens the mood with an interruption—a phone call from a certain Mrs. Doorn, the wife of George's former chiropractor, who has run off to Las Vegas with an ice skater. The lonely lady is "asking him for a date," which enables Simon to have George refuse with some very funny lines. He says:

Well, yes, in a manner of speaking, we are in the same boat, but we don't necessarily have to paddle together. I think we have to go up our own streams.... Well, yes, it is possible that we could meet up river one day. I don't rule that out.

Meanwhile, Leo has come in and quips, "Is that from *The African Queen?*" George, completely in character, opts for an honest refusal rather than giving the lady "a line," as his brother suggests, although he agrees with Leo's observation that "Next to Christmas, loneliness is the biggest business in America." George is somewhat shocked by this call and by other invitations that have been proffered him by solitary women, whereas Leo states flatly that *he* would be more than willing to accept any and all comers, if only Marilyn, his wife, would understand. He concedes that all this loneliness is sad, but retorts smartly:

> Now if you want to feel sorry for yourself and everyone else in the world who's suffered a loss, that's your concern. It's my job to brighten up the place. I am God's interior decorator and he has sent me to paint you two coats of happiness.

At this point the playwright inserts some humorous interchange between the brothers about a date Leo had recently arranged for George with a certain Bambi, "a jazzy blonde who dyes a zigzag streak of dark blue in her hair and wears an electric dress!" It is not surprising, therefore, that George cannot be persuaded to listen to Leo's talk of his latest "find." It is in this scene too that George says, "There are no more Barbaras left in the world.... If you meet them *once* in your life, God has been more than good to you," a statement that will become particularly meaningful in understanding George's guilt feelings when it seems that God has been good to him twice. Nevertheless, Leo, the undying optimist, insists on leaving the telephone number of this "Miss Serious," just in case George should change his mind.

In scene 4 Jennie is packing to go "home" to Cleveland for a short visit. Faye finds this timing very unfortunate because an old flame, one Leo Schneider, has promised to have his recently widowed brother, George, call Jennie for a date. This exchange, of course, gives the playwright the opportunity to parallel George's refusal with Jennie's. As she tells Faye, she has had it with men who "greet me at the door with a silk shirt unbuttoned to a tanned navel, chest hair neatly combed and wearing more jewelry than me." But Faye, like her counterpart, Leo, believes that it is her mission to arrange the lives of others—to "make them happy"—and she is infuriated as Jennie exits without answering the ringing telephone.

When we see George again, two weeks later, in scene 5, he is calling his brother to ask for the telephone number of an elderly retired librarian, who may be helpful in some research. Stretching coincidence a bit, he finds what he believes to be this Serene Jurgens's number, but reaches Jennie's number instead, just as she returns from her trip. The confusion between Serene, aged eighty-five, and Jennie, aged thirty-two, is amusing, and although Jennie tells George flatly that she's not interested in dating, there is unmistakable rapport for several call-backs, so the two finally agree to meet for a "five-minute-look," just to satisfy "the pushers," Leo and Faye. George then leaves for Jennie's apartment, where scene 6 takes place.

As one would expect, both of these very sensitive people find themselves embarrassed by the meeting that had seemed such a good idea twenty minutes earlier, but they do hit it off and make a "regulation date" for the following evening. In this scene too Simon lets the audience know that Gus Hendricks, Jennie's first husband, had left pro football after only one season and had then been "in mutual funds, the saloon business, broadcasting, and sports promotion," all within a period of three months. As Jennie puts it, "he had some problems." George too is more clearly defined as an author who writes two kinds of novels: those in Column A are spy novels, written under a hyphenated name (to sound English) for money, whereas those in Column B are "good" novels, written under his own name for posterity. This revelation may have some significance in relation to Simon's own work, since up to this point he is usually spoken of as the "most successful American playwright," an evaluation clearly referring to the box office appeal of his plays, with his more serious value generally overlooked. In any case, these two people seem almost at once to have not only an attraction for each other, but also an ease of manner with each other which bodes well for their future relationship, and the scene closes with George leaving on the comic line, "I can't believe you're from the same man who gave us Bambi."

Scene 7 is very brief and expository, its only purpose to make clear to the audience how Jennie feels. She admits to Faye that she's been seeing a lot of George Schneider, and that although she can't quite believe it herself, she feels that she's genuinely in love with him after only one week. Faye, in contrast, jokes about her miserable marriage. Sidney's ear problems, she says, have thrown him off balance. "He keeps rolling away from me in bed." Like Jennie, Faye is an actress, working at the moment in a TV soap opera, and she cracks, "It's a very sad state of affairs when things are worse at home than they are on the soap...." So we get the contrast between Jennie and Faye paralleling that between George and Leo.

In the very crucial scene 8, which takes place later that night, Simon gets to his major theme as the two protagonists relate to each other in a way that is central to the personality and feelings of each. George has become inexplicably ill during dinner; Jennie is genuinely solicitous and loving. But it is very obvious that although George returns her feelings, he is not successfully dealing with the guilt engendered by his caring. He says:

> I keep trying to push Barbara out of my mind...I can't do it. I've tried, Jennie...I don't really want to. I'm so afraid of losing her forever....I know I'll never stop loving Barbara, but I feel so good about you...and I can't get the two things together in my mind.

Jennie is completely supportive and assures George that she will simply stand by and help him accept *all* his feelings, and the scene ends on a light romantic note as he offer to show her his apartment, starting with the bedroom. In typical Simonesque fashion, he says, "Sure. I pass out at fish. What have you got to be afraid of?"

Three days later, in scene 9, George is trying to tell his brother that he has decided to marry Jennie at once, but he finds that Leo is hardly listening, being concerned instead with his own imminently dissolving marriage. Marilyn wants to leave him, he says, and although there are laugh-lines here—for example, she will wait until after their daughter's Thursday night appearance in the school play, *Pinocchio,* and "the kid isn't even playing the lead. She's a herring that gets swallowed by the whale."—Leo soon gets down to his gut feelings about being married, a speech that is completely consistent with his philosophy of life and love, as he asserts with some conviction:

> The trouble with marriage is that it's relentless. Every morning when you wake up, it's still there. If I could just get a leave of absence every once in a while. A two-week leave of absence. I used to get them all the time in the Army and I always came back.

He complains that Marilyn has no imagination, that they're stagnating after eleven years in their "comfortable little house in the country," but it becomes evident that he is simply not a viable candidate for monogamy, for whatever reason, as he admits openly to Faye later.

In strong contrast, George is supremely confident that he's doing the right thing in planning to marry Jennie without delay. He tells Leo that he and Barbara had known each other for only eight weeks and that he could have married her after their third date. Now, miraculously, he feels the same way about Jennie. Leo suggests that some less permanent arrangement might be preferable for the time being, and finally gets George's permission to have a talk with Jennie. The sense of deep love between the two men is clearly shown, while at the same time their basic attitudes are sharply contrasted as Leo exits with the wisecrack, "I don't know what the hell I'm doing in publicity. I was born to be a Jewish mother." George then telephones Jennie to tell her of Leo's impending visit, inadvertently verbalizing some of his own doubts when he kiddingly asks her first to wait (she says fine), then to move in with him (she agrees), and, finally to be ready for their wedding on the following Monday. The scene and act close with Jennie "looking thoughtful" and George looking at a framed photo of his first wife.

Act II opens with George on the telephone explaining his forthcoming marriage to his mother, who is in Florida, as Jennie enters with a gift—his two serious novels bound in leather, "guaranteed to last as long as Dickens and Twain." He gives her an engagement ring, and the scene ends on a comic note as George talks to his mother, saying, "What else am I doing? You mean besides getting married? Well, I bought a new sports jacket —grey.... You can never have too much grey, Mom." This interlude provides some comic relief, but is in no sense an obligatory scene.

Scene 2 reverts to Jennie's as her friend Faye asks for a key. She intends to "have an affair," but since her reluctance is obvious and this kind of episode is very much against Jennie's idea of a wise way to assuage frustration, she tries to dissuade the unhappy Faye, but does give her a key. Almost as soon as Faye has gone, Leo comes somewhat apologetically to "state his case" to Jennie. In a speech that seems a little out of character for the wisecracking Leo, he says:

> Listen, I once did some work for an insurance company and they published these statistics...the greatest loss that can happen to a man or woman, in terms of traumatic impact to the survivor, is the death of a spouse....The loss of a parent, a child, a job, a house, any catastrophe, was not deemed as devastating as the death of a husband or wife. In time, thank God and the laws of nature, most people work through it....But it needs the time. And I wouldn't want you and George to be hurt because that time was denied to him...to both of you.

Jennie then asks Leo to tell her how it was when Barbara died, and in Leo's description the playwright gives his audience what is probably one of the two most personal and poignant revelations in the play. He explains how George had refused at first to believe that Barbara was terminally ill, how he had finally accepted her passing without even the slightest sign of a breakdown, and then had cracked up completely at one fell swoop. Finally, he had gone into therapy, but after one month had decided not to go back. Leo says:

> He wouldn't explain why. I called the doctor and he explained to me that George was making a very determined effort not to get

better...because getting better meant that he was ready to let go
of Barbara and there was no way he was going to let that happen.

He then goes on to explain how he had tried in his own way to
help George return to life after the trip to Europe, coming full cir-
cle to George's meeting with Jennie.

Jennie's first reaction is anger, then fear. As she puts it:

> I've just come from five years of analysis and a busted marriage.
> I couldn't believe how *lucky* I was when George came into my life
> ...that he was going to make everything all right...And look at
> me...I'm so damned nervous everything might fall apart. It all
> feels like it's hanging by a string and this sharp pair of scissors is
> coming toward me—snapping away.

But she assures Leo that even if everything isn't all right, she will
make it right, and the scene closes with the feeling that all will be
well.

In scene 3 the nervous bridegroom and his brother are engaged in a rather humorous conversation about the impending
ceremony, but just beneath the surface there is a sense of
George's inner conflict and possibly even a foreshadowing of
near tragedy. As he exits, George quips, "You were right, Leo.
It's all too soon. I should have waited until eleven, eleven-thirty.
Ten o'clock is too soon."

Scene 4 takes place in Jennie's, where Faye in a sexy black
negligee is nervously awaiting a lover, and simultaneously in
George's, where a near-frantic Leo enters to reveal that *he* is that
chosen man. He dials Jennie's phone and explains:

> I can't meet you now. I've got to rush back out to the airport.
> George forgot the airline tickets and his travelers' checks, the
> limousine had a flat on the Long Island Expressway, and
> Jennie's got the heaves....I've got to run. There are two people
> about to leave for their honeymoon who aren't talking to each
> other.

As a comic tag to the scene, Simon has Faye say, "This is
definitely my last affair."

The returning honeymooners, in scene 5, illuminate sharply the salient point of the play. They are glum, silent, rain-soaked in body and spirit, and very tense. Jennie's jokes, which arise to an extent from the eight glasses of wine she has had enroute home (George has meticulously kept count), simply do not go over with her husband, who is trying very hard to avoid what he feels might be a confrontation that could damage their relationship permanently. But Jennie will not allow him the luxury of avoidance; in her own past she has been unable to handle conflict, but now she's determined—wisely or not—to see this through at whatever cost. It is evident that they should have talked of their past loves and marriages before being coupled, but at this stage of the proceedings there seems, at least to Jennie, no other way of handling the present except to unlock the vault, take out the past and examine it—hating it (as she does) or idolizing it (as George does)—but looking at it in either case.

Her point is well taken, of course, since what she proposes is living in the present—not ignoring the past, but accepting it as experience through which to grow. George is not really upset at Jennie, although he does hit out at her with belittling remarks, such as, "I noticed you sitting on the plane with the pen poised over *The New York Times* crossword puzzle for three and a half hours without ink ever once touching paper." The real target of his anger is George Schneider. As he says, he expects of himself a full commitment to her—to their marriage—and somehow it just doesn't happen. Every effort Jennie makes to "understand" just infuriates him further until she says that she will not try to be Barbara just to make their marriage work. George is driven to a cruelty almost beyond bounds as he tells her, "You're not Barbara. That's clear enough." No matter how Jennie reacts, George will not, cannot, overcome the negative feelings he expresses in this second significant revelation:

> I resent you for *everything!* I don't feel like making you happy tonight...I don't feel like having a wonderful time....I don't think I *wanted* a "terrifically wonderful honeymoon!"...I resent everything you want out of marriage that I've already had... And for making me reach so deep inside to give it to you again. I resent being at L or M and having to go back to A!...And most

of all, I resent not being able to say in front of you that I miss
Barbara so much....

He then covers his eyes and cries silently, closing the scene as he
leaves Jennie alone onstage with the line, "As they say in the
trade, we got problems, kid."

In scene 6 the sub-plot resumes with Faye and Leo in Jennie's
apartment. Their attempt at an "affair" has been abruptly interrupted by a phone call which Leo had felt compelled to accept
from his "biggest client." Not only is Faye understandably upset
because he'd given out the number, but also she is beside herself
at being made to feel so cheap because of his casual attitude.
Somehow they begin to move toward each other again, by dancing, and Faye tells him that he's too experienced at this business
of adultery—he must have done it many times before. Leo finally
admits that she is correct, but then comes on with a very accurate
observation of his own. He tells her that she doesn't have enough
reason to be here at all. Faye then confesses that what she wants
isn't an "affair"; it's the excitement of being *in love* again. Like
Barney Cashman in *Last of the Red Hot Lovers,* this character
seems to feel that life is going by so fast that she may become old
and "interesting looking" (instead of beautiful) without ever
having experienced a genuine romance. Since these two had
known each other twelve years earlier, when both were single,
Faye asks Leo what he thinks would have happened if they had
married each other, and he tells her it would have worked out
beautifully. When she accuses him of lying, however, he agrees
that he's only told her what she'd wanted to hear. His next speech
is completely revealing and rounds out the inner man only
glimpsed in earlier scenes with his brother. He says:

> I need something new. It's why I like show business. There's
> another opening every three weeks. I can't be monogamous,
> Faye. What can I do? Take shots for it? But in our system I'm
> put down as a social criminal. I can't be faithful to my wife and I
> hate the guilt that comes with playing around. So I compromise.
> I have lots of unpleasurable affairs...And what makes it worse,
> I really do care for Marilyn. I can't stop and I don't expect her to
> understand. So we end up hurting each other. I don't like it,

Faye. I don't like crawling into bed at two o'clock in the morning and feeling the back of a cold, angry woman.... And I don't like you coming up here under any false pretenses. I would love to make love to you, but that's the end of the sentence. I don't want a fine romance. I don't want to dance on the ceiling or have my heart stand still when "she" walks in the door. Because I really don't want to hurt anyone anymore. All I want is a little dispassionate passion. Let George and Jennie handle all the romance for the East Coast. The man is half crazed right now and he's welcome to it. I'll tell you what I *do* want, Faye...I want a woman who looks exactly like you and feels like you and thinks exactly like me.

There are unmistakable echoes here of Elaine Navazio *(Last of the Red Hot Lovers),* who more or less says the same thing to Barney Cashman, and it would seem that from Simon's point of view these kinds of people, who consciously accept life only at the hedonistic level, border on being genuinely tragic characters. All of their attempts at skimming life without emotional commitment seems futile. True, they do avoid emotional depths, but by implication, they avoid emotional heights as well, and ironically, do not seem content at their chosen levels either.

In order to maintain the comic mode, the playwright then has these two agree to be "friends," with Faye saying, "I'll be damned if I'm going home empty-handed.... Give me one warm, passionate, and very sincere kiss." Leo is happy to grant this request, and somehow they end up on the bed just as Jennie walks in. After a few embarrassing moments, Jennie leaves followed quickly by Leo, who slams the door and ends the scene with, "That's a first for me. That has never happened before. Never caught by a sister-in-law. *Never!*"

In scene 7 Jennie returns to George's apartment, to find him packed and about to leave for Los Angeles to do a film of one of his spy novels. She is furious at his "leaving her with all his memories," and after almost coming to physical blows, Jennie explodes:

You know what you want better than me, George. I don't know what you expect to find out there except a larger audience for your two shows a day of suffering. . . . I know I'm not as smart as you. Maybe I can't analyze and theorize and speculate on why we behave as we do and react as we do and suffer guilt and love and hate. . . . But there's one thing I *do* know. . . . I know how I *feel.* I know that I can stand here watching you try to destroy everything I've ever wanted in my life, wanting to smash your face with my fists because you won't even make the slightest effort to opt for happiness—and still know that I love you. That's always so clear to me. It's the one place I get all my strength from. . . . You mean so much to me that I am willing to take all your abuse and insults and insensitivity because that's what you need to do to prove I'm not going to leave you. I can't promise I'm not going to die, George, that's asking too much. But if you want to test me, go ahead and test me. You want to leave, leave! But *I'm* not the one who's going to walk away. . . .

She continues, explaining that she feels good about herself and if he's fool enough to walk away from a wonderful person like her that's his problem. And ends by saying that if he wants her, he should fight for her, because she's fighting like hell for him.

George's reaction is reassuring. He says that he's glad she's on *his* side, and he admits that he loves her very much. However, his problem is not solved that simply. As he puts it:

I want to walk over now and take you in may arms and say, "Okay, we're finished with the bad part. Now, what's for dinner?" but I'm stuck, Jennie. . . . I'm just stuck some place in my mind, and it's driving me crazy. Something is keeping me here, glued to this spot like a big, dumb, overstuffed chair.

At this point it is clear that all will be well; however, George does feel he has to go to Los Angeles to try to "get unstuck," to get rid of his self-pity. Jennie agrees, asking only to move back to her apartment temporarily while he's away.

Scene 8 finds Faye opening Jennie's door to Leo who has come to retrieve his wallet left behind in his hurried exit the day before. They chat, and Faye tells him that she's going to see Jennie's psychiatrist. She then asks what he's doing about his "problems." Typically, Leo answers, "Nothing! I have no intention of changing. So why should I pay some doctor to make me feel guilty about it?'' She asks him if he and Marilyn are going to separate, to which he fliply replies, ''Yes. But not this year. We have too many dinner dates.'' Somehow, at the end of their conversation, these two decide to complete their interrupted kiss (from scene 6) just as Jennie walks in from the shower. This brings comic relief, and Leo exits on the line, ''Jesus, life was so simple when we were kids. No matter how much trouble you got into outside, when you got home, you always got a cupcake.'' Faye then tells Jennie that her attempt at an affair with Leo was only ''practicing with someone she knew''; the one she really lusted after was Jennie's ex-husband, Gus. And again a bit reminiscent of Barney Cashman, calling his wife, Thelma, at the end of *Last of the Red Hot Lovers,* Faye says that she and her husband, Sidney, have decided to try an adult motel in New Jersey. ''From now on,'' she explains,'' I'm only cheating with the immediate family.''

In the final scene of *Chapter Two* (scene 9) George returns and tries to telephone Jennie, whose line is busy because she's trying to reach him in Los Angeles. When he does get through, they almost repeat the earlier scene with the ''Serene Jurgens routine,'' but then become rather serious as George tells his wife that he had become ''unstuck'' in the Los Angeles Airport and has come back to New York to ''embrace his happiness.'' He tells her also that he had finished the last chapter of his new book on the plane and is reading it to her—so as ''not to lose the momentum,'' he says, as the play ends:

> It's called *Falling into Place,* dedicated to Jennie, a nice girl to spend the rest of your life with. Chapter One...Walter Maslanski looked in the mirror and saw what he feared most, Walter Maslanski. Not that Walter's features were awesome by any means. He had the sort of powder-puff eyes that could be stared down in an abbreviated battle by a one-eyed senior citizen canary....

Curtain.

In *Chapter Two* Neil Simon seems to have kept quite well within the criteria set down earlier: he has written a comedy with believable characters who bring alive a very important idea or

theme. If the laughter is gentler than in some of his plays, if the
farcical element is almost entirely missing, if he has grown
beyond using the running gag, it is all to the good. What may
have hampered his usual method of having characters "work out
their own logical destinies" is the simple fact that certain
elements of the main plot had actually taken place before the
writing. In "real life" the playwright had two partially grown
daughters to consider when making the second marriage, but
Simon elected to make George a childless widower. In "real life"
George's brother would be somewhat his senior, not two years
his junior. And in "real life" the entire sub-plot probably never
happened. What the playwright wants to do—and does do very
successfully—is to use his own bereavement almost metaphor-
ically to stress the universal significance of never cutting oneself
off from life either through self-pity or guilt.

There are undeniably some parallels with earlier plays, particularly since Simon has created characters who are capable of
love and characters who have decided to forego that ecstacy, as
discussed in regard to *The Last of the Red Hot Lovers*. He ex-
hibits his usual benign attitude toward human beings, albeit he
acknowledges their imperfections. And he remains very much a
spokesman for moderation, monogamy, and magnanimity. If he
feels that those people who refuse to commit themselves without
reserve are near-tragic, he nevertheless respects their right to live
their own lives as they choose, merely hinting that they do not
need to be "punished" by other people (or by any higher power)
since they are quite apt to punish themselves in one way or
another. As Faye Medwick says when she makes her final exit,
"There's a lesson to be learned from all this.... I wonder what
the hell it is."

If there are minor inconsistencies—such as Jennie, supposedly a Bennington girl, saying at one point that she "hasn't read all
those books," and a little manipulation, such as George's finding
Jennie's number written on the back of the paper with that of the
elderly librarian, or Leo's running into Faye, Sidney, and Jennie
at the 21 Club—these can be overlooked when the play is considered as a total theatrical experience. The difficulty of eighteen
scenes is smoothly overcome by the simultaneous staging too.

What is most remarkable about *Chapter Two* is the way in which Simon has characterized George Schneider so clearly that his loss and eventual recovery become symbolic of universal bereavement and then renewal. Bereavement does not always involve the final fact of death, of course; perhaps every adult at some time in his life has experienced an irreversible loss of a loved one and has faced a time of mourning. In this sense, then, most members of the audience can identify with George. Simon, however, does not stop there. He goes on to a genuinely "happy ending" beyond mere theatrical convention by posing a solution: acknowledge the fact fully, but do not cling to it self-pityingly nor with guilt. Instead go on to Chapter Two with complete acceptance of and openness to life.

Summing Up

It is by no means an original notion that the comic genre has been effectively used as a form through which serious ideas may be presented. The point of this study, however, has not been to discuss this proposition as a generality, but rather to validate specifically the fact the *Neil Simon* has accomplished this feat with consummate skill, and to illustrate by analysis some of the means he has employed. There is, of course, no way to pinpoint precisely the components of any artist's talent; nevertheless, certain features of Simon's work are salient and can be labeled common threads which run through the thirteen plays considered here.

First, in keeping with the classic writers of comedy from the time of Menander, he is categorically opposed to every form of extremism and frequently takes the opportunity through his characters to suggest that Aristotle's "golden mean" is the ideal. The desirability of taking the "middle way," rather than clinging to an immoderate posture is made very clear in every play from *Come Blow Your Horn* (to enjoy life one does not need to be completely hedonistic) through *California Suite* (all "life" doesn't necessarily reside on one coast or the other), although it is not always the main theme, as it is in *Barefoot in the Park,* and, to an even greater degree, in *The Odd Couple.* It is true also that modern urban society tends to tolerate and even to encourage behavior far from the "golden mean," such as the collecting of needless "garbage" as evidence of affluence in *Prisoner of Second Avenue,* and where this occurs, the playwright's tone makes it very clear that he is less permissive toward society as a whole than toward individuals who ineptly but sincerely try to cope with its vagaries.

Next, we should examine the assertion made by the Narrator
(Writer) in the sketch "Surgery" (*The Good Doctor*) to the effect
that laughter is based on other people's pain. To some extent this
is true, and, theoretically, farce which depends heavily on
physical action, does involve, at least potentially, suffering in this
sense. But it is important to note that in Simon's plays it is not
really so much the pain itself which is the evocator, as it is the incongruity which triggers that pain. For instance, if we look at
Mrs. Baker's rather trivial "pain" (*Come Blow Your Horn*)
because she can't find a pencil with which to take messages, we
can see that it is really because we *expect* pencils which do not
materialize (until Buddy finds a container full a little later) that
we laugh, and not at Mrs. Baker's frustration and tears. Even in
"Surgery" itself, it is not the patient's agony which we find
amusing, but the fact that under "normal" circumstances we
would expect a dentist (even a trainee) to be able to remove a
tooth without ending up in a wrestling match with his patient. So,
it is the contradiction of the expected which makes the scene
hilarious, not the man's pain. Again, near the close of *Prisoner
of Second Avenue,* when the water has been turned off in the
Edisons' apartment building, it is quite surprising that the irate
neighbor upstairs has "saved" some water with which she
drenches Mel, ironically just as he is apologizing for Edna's outburst of temper. What we laugh at here, then, is the incongruity
of her *having* water, rather than Mel's humiliation. When this
technique is applied to a character, such as Sidney Lipton in
God's Favorite, we laugh because it is very doubtful that such a
man would be employed even by Western Union; yet Simon
makes this inept bungler the messenger of God!

It is important to make this distinction between laughter at
the pain of others and laughter at underlying incongruity in
Simon's work because one of his hallmarks is his great compassion for his fellow human beings, which precludes his soliciting
laughter in direct proportion to the hurt suffered by his
"people." In the plays where there is authentic pain, as in
Gingerbread Lady, several playlets in both *Plaza Suite* and
California Suite, portions of *Prisoner of Second Avenue, The
Sunshine Boys,* and *Chapter Two,* there is no attempt at humor at

all—just genuine feeling without sentimentality.[1]

Another thread which runs through all of Simon's work is a basic respect and regard for the institution which gives stability to society—the family. Even when there are contemplated or temporary lapses in marital fidelity; even when one or the other partner is less than the ideal husband or wife; even when the children are "disappointing" to their parents, the playwright implies that the monogamous family unit is of paramount importance and should be preserved if at all possible. At the same time, he does not hesitate to make us aware through his characters' dilemmas in this area that this institution is often in sad need of repair—but repair doesn't mean demolishment.

One of the most effective techniques Neil Simon uses in a number of his plays is the pointing out of human limitation—the contrast between intention and execution. This not only works well in that it enables audiences to laugh at themselves without being consciously impelled to acknowledge the target—since human limitation is such a universal characteristic—but it also serves to develop certain characters most graphically. A prime example is Barney Cashman (*Last of the Red Hot Lovers*) whose earnest and repeated attempts to exceed his "limitations" are as fruitless as his attempts to stop the smell of fish from returning to his hands each afternoon, "like the incoming tide."

Another consideration in Neil Simon's work must be the matter of language. He relies neither on the play-on-words (the pun) for its own sake, nor on risqué language to get laughs. But he does make good use of non sequiturs, and he also utilizes non-communication effectively. Occasionally some of his characters say silly things, such as Mrs. Baker's "I'm no going around *any* worlds..." (*Come Blow Your Horn*), or Mort Franklyn's, "I said I'd *pay* for the tennis balls, didn't I?" ("Visitors from Chicago," *California Suite*), but we are tolerant of such lines because they are done "in character," and because the humor in them stems from the illogical use of words which in another context might be perfectly reasonable. A number of his people do not talk to each other—or listen, really—and this circumstance which is so often tragic in life can be at least momentarily funny on the stage. Generally, he reproduces speech so adroitly that it almost always seems that his characters "say" exactly what they *would say* were they living human beings and not creations of the playwright's imagination. This facility with dialogue is indispensible in giving Simon's characters the plausibility which they must have for audience identification, while simultaneously eliciting laughter crucial to successful comedy.

A fine illustration of the playwright's ability to make a conversation credible and hilarious at the same time is found in *Prisoner of Second Avenue* (Act II, scene 2), when Mel's brother, Harry, and his three sisters are discussing Mel's predicament in terms of both his adult behavior and his childhood misbehavior. The women are "remembering," inaccurately, of course, symptoms from the past, whereas Harry is more concerned with the present. All of them sound authentically like concerned siblings of their sort would sound, yet they entertain us with a very funny interchange:

PAULINE: He wasn't nervous. He was high strung. Melvin was always high strung.

PEARL: I call it nervous. As a baby he was nervous, as a boy he was nervous, in the Army he was nervous. How long did he last in the Army, anyway?

JESSIE: Two weeks.

PEARL: There you are. He was nervous.

PAULINE: Where do you think nerves come from? From being high strung.

PEARL: Then why weren't any of us high strung? We all had the same parents. He was nervous, he was fidgety, he chewed fast...I never saw him swallow.

JESSIE: No one could talk to him. Poppa could never talk to him, I remember.

PAULINE: How could Poppa talk to him? Mel was three years old when Poppa died.

PEARL: If he wasn't so nervous, Poppa could have talked to him...He had the same thing in high school. A nervous breakdown in high school.

HARRY: Who you talking about?

PEARL: Mel! He had a nervous breakdown in high school. You don't remember?

HARRY: What are you talking about? He didn't have a ner-

> vous breakdown, he had a broken arm. He fell in
> the gym and broke his arm.
> PAULINE: ...Mel never had a nervous breakdown.
> PEARL: Isn't that funny, I thought he had a nervous break-
>   down. Maybe I'm thinking of somebody else.

After more of this kind of conversation, Harry finally asserts pragmatically:

> Fact number one, Mel has had a nervous breakdown. Fact
> number two, besides a nervous breakdown, Mel doesn't have a
> job. The man is totally unemployed. Fact number three, besides
> a nervous breakdown and not having a job, the man is practically
> penniless....it's none of my business how a man squandered a
> life's savings on bad investments for which he never asked *my* ad-
> vice once....My business is what are we going to do for Mel?
> How much are we going to give?

Simon follows this scrupulously "recorded" conversation with the pithy stage direction: *(The silence is deafening....After an hour of silence, Harry speaks again)*...Well? [Enough said.]

As to the matter of plot, even when the plays become somewhat farcical, so that coincidences are acceptable, or even when Simon seems more than remotely related to Feydeau, so that action becomes accelerated, he adheres, except in *Chapter Two,* to the single plot or story line. Generally, he stays with the concept that as the characters "live out" certain scenes—act and interact so that they command what Louis Kronenberger called "the sad fraternal smile of recognition"[2] from the audience—a logical series of events (technically a plot) will evolve naturally.

With only two exceptions—*The Star Spangled Girl* and *California Suite*—all of Simon's plays are set in New York, and this is a thread in itself, since to some degree the flavor of that city and its environment comes through quite clearly; many characters have patterns of speech which could come from no other place, and a few like Lewis and Clark (*The Sunshine Boys*) have special patterns of behavior as well. To be fair, however, other cities of considerable size might have been used instead. They key word here is *size* since it is the urban setting itself which is mandatory as the milieu in which Simon's people live.

A critical study of Neil Simon's work, then, reveals certain common elements which serve to identify the oeuvre as commercially successful comedy in which three-dimensional characters give life to themes of universal interest. Simon recognizes certain personal and societal problems; however, he never offers didactic solutions. He shows a preference for conventional moral behavior; however, he has great tolerance for mortal fallibility. He suggests mutual concession in personal relationships; however, he never "punishes" those who persist in extreme modes of behavior.

Above all, his plays which may appear simple to those who never look beyond the fact that they are amusing are, in fact, frequently more perceptive and revealing of the human condition than many plays labeled complex dramas. To quote Horace Walpole: "Life is a comedy to the man who thinks, a tragedy to the man who feels."[3] To Neil Simon, who thinks *and* feels, the comic form provides a means to present serious subjects so that audiences may laugh to avoid weeping.

1. Even the few truly stupid people who come off like caricatures rather than characters (Sophie Rauschmeyer in *The Star Spangled Girl,* for example) are never ridiculed or "hurt" to elict audience laughter at their expense.

2. Introduction to *Cavalcade of Comedy,* edited by Louis Kronenberger, Simon and Schuster, New York, 1953.

3. Letter to the Countess of Upper Ossory, 16 August, 1776.

Index